DESIGNER ACCESSORIES TO MAKE FOR YOUR HOME

35 EASY, INEXPENSIVE WAYS TO COMPLEMENT ANY ROOM

by Louis Nichole

Butterick Publishing

To my mother and father

Printed in the United States of America

Book design by Sheila Lynch
Illustrations by Mel Klapholtz
All photographs by the author

DESIGNER ACCESSORIES TO MAKE FOR YOUR HOME

Tongue Depressor Planter Variation, page 57

Contents

List of Color Photographs

Introduction

- Do you feel you are among the last of America's creative homemakers?
- Each month, do projects in consumer and decorating magazines entice and excite you as you leaf through their pages?
- Suddenly, do all your latent energies and hidden creativities restlessly begin to surge forth and explode?
- Are you then determined to attempt these fabulous creations and turn your home into a decorator's delight?
- And does the enthusiasm die when you turn the page because you think that you don't have the talent, money, or materials to do all that?

If you have answered yes to any of the above, this is the book you've waited for. Here is a book with everything that you always wanted to design but were afraid to try or thought you couldn't afford. These designs have been tested throughout New England since 1973 in demonstration workshops I present for people with no design experience.

The contents of this book can help you give your home a charming, personal look. And if you happen to have champagne taste but a beer pocketbook, don't be discouraged. You can make many of these projects by using such inexpensive, everyday ingredients as cornstarch, hand cream, Styrofoam, pipe cleaners, paint cans, and instant coffee.

The book is divided into five chapters. Chapter 1 reveals everything that you need to know to complete any project in this book easily and successfully. Chapter 2, "A Country Collection," presents designs reminiscent of Early Americana with a flavor that is fresh, clean, and unmistakably "country." Chapter 3, "Nature's Own," contains designs made from dried and natural materials, most of which are available free in forest or wooded areas. Chapter 4, "A Holiday Collection," recalls the charm of holidays past with designs that reflect the spirit of the Colonial, Federal, and Victorian periods. And finally, Chapter 5 tells you how to make what you've made look even better. Designer secrets show how easily a merely handsome wreath can be transformed into a wonderfully dramatic display, simply by adding accessories and lighting.

So there you are. There's nothing to stop you now. Here is everything that you always wanted to make but were afraid to try because you thought you couldn't—but you really can.

ONE

What You'll Need And How To Use It

THIS IS THE EVERYTHING-you-wanted-to-know chapter—the hows and how-not-tos, the wheres and where-not-tos. A basic understanding of techniques, design, where to get supplies, and how to use them correctly is essential to success in completing any project included in this book.

This chapter is divided into three parts. The first deals with glue, adhesives, and fasteners—explaining what they are and how to use them effectively. "Floral materials," the second part, explains some of the fundamental florist supplies and types of dried materials. You can get many of these absolutely free in various places such as wooded areas—or your local cemetery dump. The third part, consisting of technique notes, incorporates information from the other parts of the chapter, showing how to put your entire design together. Read the whole chapter thoroughly and familiarize yourself with the skills and techniques. Refer back to any section as you need to when you do a specific project. All the tricks of the trade are important if a project is to be completed easily and successfully.

Materials

GLUE, ADHESIVES, AND FASTENERS

Floral Glue and other Instant-Contact Glues

The glue that I have used in all these projects is Oasis floral glue, which was originally produced especially for the decorator, designer, and florist trades. It is the only instant-contact floral glue that I know of, and it adapts most successfully to craft items. It produces a tough, lasting bond, cutting your project time in half. Oasis glue works with fabric, ribbons, trims, dried and natural materials, Styrofoam, glass, paper, and pottery, among other materials. People tell me that they have used it on anything from last-minute hems to torn-off heels. It is more expensive than other glues, but it is well worth the price. It is available—not in dumps unfortunately—in many nurseries and florist shops. You may find other glues under other brand names in various parts of the country. I mention Oasis only because I am familiar with it, and do not intend to endorse it over any other similar product. If you use another glue, make sure it can bond the materials you are working with instantly.

Floral glue should be used very sparingly. The less you use, the quicker it bonds. Always remove the excess glue from the brush along the rim of the can, so as not to drip any glue on your project. Use a light "dry-brush technique," wiping the brush along the surface of what you're gluing.

Keep glue covered when not in use; if you don't, it will thicken and harden into a single lump. Always close the cover tight, and keep the container in an unpright position. You can remove glue from your hands with nail polish remover.

Floral Tape

This kind of tape is used to cover exposed stems, wires, and picks. It performs two functions: it reinforces a stem or wire and hides any exposed wires that might be distracting in an arrangement. The covered wires blend into the foundation of the arrangement. You can use

12

green floral tape when ferns or greens are the foundation; white or brown tape on dried or natural materials. Floral tape is readily available in dime stores, craft shops, and nurseries.

Using Floral Tape. There is one simple and very important thing to remember when you use floral tape: stretch your tape before you use it. For the beginner, this is the most effective way for best results.

1. After you stretch your tape, starting at the top, wrap a small piece of it around your item (Figure A).

2. Pinch the tape together with your two fingers (the moisture in your fingers is enough to bond it together).

3. Angling the tape in a downward direction, wrap the tape around the item, allowing the ends of the tape to overlap slightly with the row above (Figure B). The greater the angle of the tape, the quicker, neater, and firmer is the result. By stretching and pulling the tape as you go along, you will achieve a smooth and securely taped item (Figure C).

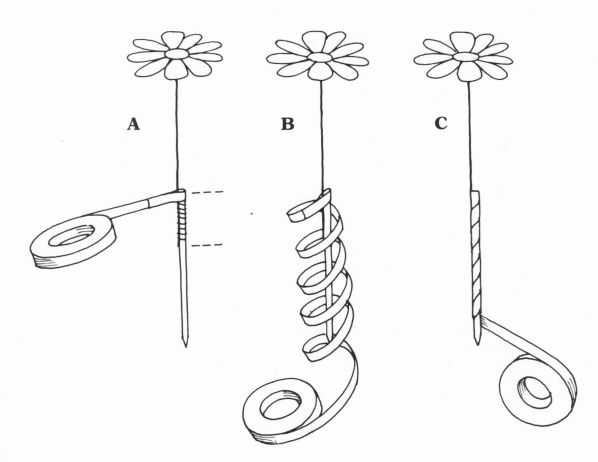

A   B   C

Florist Picks

These are thin green sticks that come in different lengths (3″, 4″, and 6″ are the most common) with a wire attached to the top. Florist picks are used to hold greens, dried materials, flowers, and other items securely into Styrofoam. The most economical place to obtain picks is at your local cemetery dump. Should you decide to purchase these picks, you can find them in most dime stores, craft shops, and nurseries that carry them in assorted sizes. Don't go to a florist to buy florist picks because you'll probably pay more.

Using Picks. Picking is important and should be done correctly.

1. Place the stem of the item you wish to pick approximately one third of the way down from the top of the pick (Figure A).

2. Wrap the wire from the pick around the stem angling the wire in a downward direction (Figure B).

3. Allow a piece of wire to remain to wrap onto the pick below the stem (Figure C). Here is where most people make their mistake. Unless the wire ends onto the pick, both the stem and the pick will separate with a small tug. You have become a successful picker if the pick and stem do not separate when you pull on them. For additional strength, wrap floral tape around the wired stem and pick (see page 13).

Wire

The following guide will help you determine the general sizes of the different gauges of wire. Choose a gauge that fits into the general category called for in each project.

Thin wire	No. 25—No. 30 gauge
Medium wire	No. 21—No. 24 gauge
Heavy wire	No. 20—No. 15 gauge

I usually use floral wire, available in green or silver, and usually sold in 18″ lengths. I find it is easier to work with than wire on a spool, since it accepts any design or form you shape it to. If you can't find a particular gauge, or if you already have another gauge, remember that thin wire is fine and very flexible; medium wire (used most

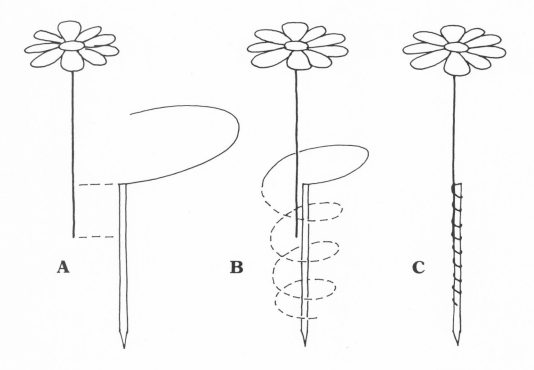

A   B   C

often) is heavier and is used for tasks such as general wiring, bow making, and reinforcement; heavy wire is often used as support and as stems, or to wire objects that are large and heavy. The exact gauge doesn't matter that much. Floral wire is available in most craft and hobby shops, nurseries, and display stores. Any wire can be purchased in hardware, lumber, or dime stores.

Using Wire. When twisting wire, most people use either hand pliers or the ever popular "finger and nail" procedure. One invaluable technique that you probably won't find in any other design book is "how to wire easily." It's such a simple skill that you might think I was really foolish to even mention it. But once you've tried this procedure, you'll seldom touch another pair of pliers. And you'll cut your project time in half.

1. Cut a length of wire and place the object to be wired in the center of the wire (Figure A).

2. Wrap the wire around the object until the wire meets (Figure B). At that point, make one twist (Figure C).

3. Here's the secret. Do not continue to twist the wire at that point. Rather, place the two ends of the wire in your hand, holding them together.

4. Rotate both hands quickly across the wire in a clockwise, circular direction (Figure D). The initial twist becomes tighter and firmer without the use of pliers or tools (Figure E). Four to five turns should be sufficient. Too many turns cause the wire to snap and break. This wiring technique applies especially well to wiring pinecones and making bows.

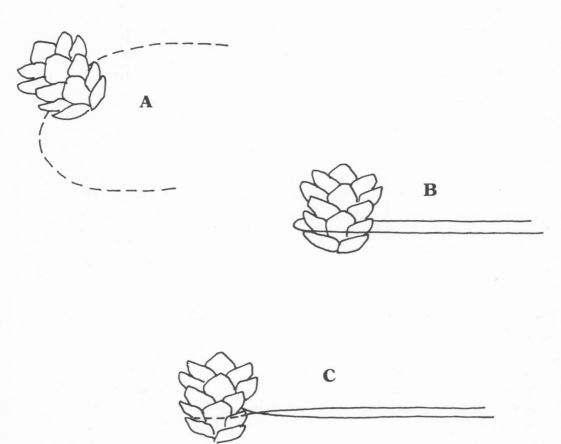

A

B

C

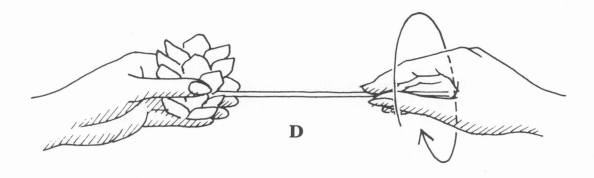

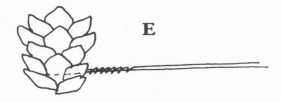

FLORAL MATERIALS

Baby's Breath

Baby's Breath is known more formally as gypsophila, and in the design trade it's called "gyp" for short. Even if you don't know the first thing about design, you can assert your knowledge at your local nursery by asking for "dried gyp." not baby's breath. Try not to buy gyp at department stores or florist shops; roadside stands and nurseries tend to be much less expensive.

Always purchase good-quality gyp. The stems should be plentiful, with many small, off-white flowers. All gyp sheds slightly. Because it tends to be very brittle and dry, it's usually best to dampen it with a small spray gun or mister, and then let it stand 10 to 15 minutes before using it. The additional moisture helps to eliminate excess shedding and makes the branches much easier to manipulate in an arrangement.

Statice

There are two kinds of statice. *German statice*, imported from Germany, is usually very white and usually remains white for several years. It is the kind of statice I recommend. *California statice* is usually fuller than German statice, and therefore less is required. Unfortunately, it is more brittle and discolors more quickly than German statice.

Statice, like gyp, can be dampened with water in order to make it easier to work with. Most of the designs in this book that incorporate gyp start with a foundation of statice.

Statice does not shed like gyp and is easier to work with. It covers more surface area because of its thickness. It is less expensive than gyp, and if you use statice, you won't have to use as much gyp. Because of its body, statice gives your designs more fullness and holds your centerpiece together more firmly. Try to keep statice out of direct sunlight as this will turn it brown very quickly.

MISCELLANEOUS

Chenille

Chenille stems come in 12" lengths and in a multitude of colors. They are similar to pipe cleaners except that chenille pile is more luxurious. Chenille stems are sold in fabric stores, craft and hobby shops, and nurseries.

Styrofoam

Styrofoam is the registered trademark of a kind of firm, somewhat porous, plastic foam that is manufactured by the Dow Chemical Company. The name *Styrofoam* is used throughout the book as a convenience to readers who are familiar with the term. Styrofoam easily accepts picks and stems and holds them securely in place. Green Styrofoam is used when ferns or greens are the foundation of an arrangement; white Styrofoam is used for dried and natural materials.

Styrofoam is readily available in enormous quantity and free at your local cemetery dump (see p. 31). If you want to buy it, try any dime store, craft shop, or nursery. Styrofoam is a vital ingredient in almost every project in this book.

Oasis and Sahara

These are both very porous types of floral foam (much more porous than Styrofoam) and are used solely for fresh or dried flower arrangements. Soak Oasis in water when using it for fresh flower arrangements. Use Sahara dry and only for dried or natural materials. Dry Oasis also accepts natural materials easily. In fact, Oasis was always used for dried materials until Sahara became available.

More often than not you can find some Oasis at the cemetery dump. Take only the Oasis that is not crumbling or falling apart. Again, if you decide to purchase either type of foam, they are available in most nurseries and flower shops.

You may find products like this under other brand names in various parts of the country. I mention these names because I am familiar with them, but this is in no way an endorsement of these products over any others.

Sphagnum Moss

This is a greenish brown dried moss that is available in dime stores, nurseries, garden shops, and other places. It is usually sold in "sheets" or "rolls" of moss. Most often, it is used to hide Styrofoam or Sahara in an arrangement.

Feathers

The best place to get free feathers is from a pheasant farm, a hunter, or a taxidermist. You can also buy feathers at craft and hobby shops. Should any of your feathers be ragged, bent, or squashed, simply place them over some steam from a teapot. They will not only open much more fully, but they will also straighten out, and the ragged edges will become more uniform.

19

PINECONES

Bleaching

This process applies not only to pinecones but also to anything "natural" that has not been varnished or shellacked, such as wood items, baskets, wicker, rattan, reed, nuts, and dried materials.

　　If you bleach pinecones or pinecone flowerettes, wire them before bleaching. Place the items in full-strength household bleach. Check them every few minutes until the desired lightness is achieved (5 to 12 minutes is usually sufficient.) Allow the pinecones to dry. Some pinecones will not reopen all the way. Take over where Mother Nature left off and help them to reopen by pushing the petals back before they are completely dry.

Red Spruce

Engelman Spruce

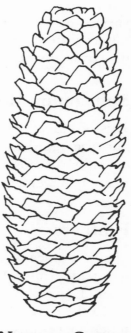

Norway Spruce

Colorado Blue Spruce

White Spruce

Douglas Fir

Scotch Pine

Sweet Gum

Eastern White Pine

Pitch Pine

Red Pine

Austrian Pine

Cleaning and Finishing

Before bleaching and finishing pinecones, you may need to remove the dried or sticky sap from the pinecones. Simply place the cones in boiling water with a small amount of detergent and bleach. The heat of the water dissolves the sap. At low heat "cook" for 10 minutes, or until you see that the sap has dissolved. Remove the cones from water. They will reopen when dry.

To give a richer luster or deeper wood finish to pinecones, use light-colored varnishes, such as light oak. Apply varnish stains with a small brush. Be careful not to use too-dark stains or varnishes, because cones will absorb too much stain and appear black.

For a brilliant, natural-looking, shine, brush cones with one or two coats of clear gloss varnish or floor sealer.

Flowerettes

Depending on the toughness or hardness of the pinecone core, two methods can be used to make pinecone flowerettes.

1. For soft cones such as in Eastern white cones, use needle-nose cutting pliers to snip off the tops of cones. Trim away any excess petals so that the flowerette is even. Depending on the desired depth of the flowerette, you may make three to four layers of petals from each pinecone. To wire, wrap wire around the last layer of petals, twisting firmly below.

2. For hard-cored cones with thick or fleshy centers, use a hacksaw blade to cut evenly down through the core. Trim off the excess petals so that the flowerette is even. You can make two to three flowerettes from each large cone. Use heavier wire to wire larger flowerettes.

GREENS

Real or Artificial Pine?

Most of the designs in Chapter 4, "The Holiday Collection," are made with real pine or other evergreens. I suggest real greens instead of plastic because the initial cost factor is much less. Besides, there is nothing like the real thing. Go to any wooded area where evergreens are plentiful. Use greens such as boxwood, pine, balsam, and hemlock: they won't shed or dry out as quickly as most other evergreens.

If you decide to use artificial greens—which can be costly—buy good-quality greens that complement your finished product.

If you like the scent and appearance of real pine but don't want the bother of having to remake a design or arrangement each year, here is a suggestion.

1. Fill two-thirds of your design with artificial greens, creating the basic shape or outline.

2. Fill in the remaining third of the design evenly with fresh evergreens.

3. Place the cut pieces on wired picks and insert into Styrofoam.

Not only does this method give your design a more natural appearance, but you can reuse the basic framework every year. When the Christmas season is over, pull out the real greens and store the project. Replace the greens the following year with fresh ones.

Technique Notes

WREATHS

There are three ways to make a pine wreath. Choose the one that is easiest for you and that applies best to your design.

Styrofoam Wreath

Because Styrofoam wreath forms are 1½" to 2" thick, they give more depth and create more fullness than wire frames. By incorporating many varieties of pine and greens (real or artificial) into your wreath, you can achieve attractive shadings and interesting texture.

    1. Cut pieces of pine and evergreen.

    2. Starting on the side of the wreath, going in one direction, insert the pine into the Styrofoam (Figure A). Secure the pine stems with greening pins (available in flower departments and florist shops), large hairpins, or heavy wire formed into loops.

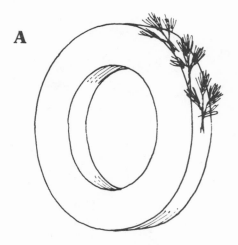

A

3. Overlap the stems from each preceding piece of pine. Follow the same procedure for the inside and top of the wreath (Figures B and C).

A quicker and easier option (and unfortunately more expensive) is to purchase a real or artificial pine or boxwood garland (usually about 8 feet long). Starting on the sides of the Styrofoam form, wrap the garland around the wreath. Continue the garland to the top and inside of the wreath. Secure the garland to the frame with wire. By using a Styrofoam foundation, you can easily insert any decoration with florist picks.

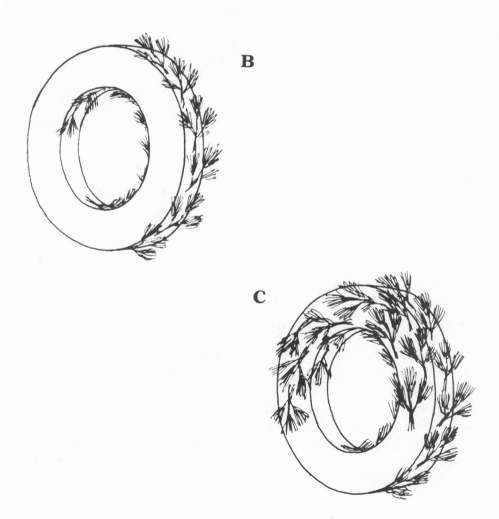

B

C

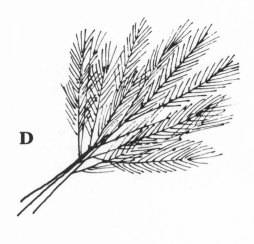

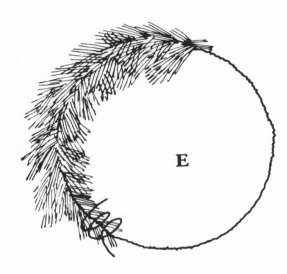

Single-Wire Frame

You can purchase this frame in almost any nursery. The final product resembles the fresh wreaths sold during the Christmas season.

1. Make clusters of assorted pine, bunching the stems tightly together (Figure D).

2. With strong wire, wire one cluster at a time, going in one direction. Overlap the stems of the preceding cluster of pine (Figure E). Follow this procedure until the wreath is complete.

Double-Wire Frame for Pinecone Wreaths

1. This frame makes a fuller wreath than the single-wire frame. Fill the inside of the wreath with running moss, cutup pieces of pine, or any other greenery. Pack the greenery tightly into the center of the frame and then wrap thin wire or string around the entire frame to hold the greens in place.

2. Cut pieces of assorted pines. Starting on the sides of the frame, going in one direction, insert the greens. Follow the same procedure for the top and inside.

CREATING A SPHERE

The Styrofoam ball is just about the quickest and easiest way to create a sphere or a semicircle. Using the ball is not a professional method, but you will be pleased with the instant success you'll achieve with it.

1. Start with a Styrofoam ball. The size of the ball you use depends on the size of your container. Try several sizes by inserting several pieces of pine or dried material into the ball. The greens should overlap the edge of your container.

2. The ball is already a shape; you simply augment it. Cut pieces of pine, greens, statice, or gyp (whatever your foundation) to approximately the same length. Adding some slightly longer length pieces creates a more interestingly shaped mound.

3. Insert the stems directly into the ball, covering two-thirds of it (Figure A). Or place your statice or gyp on 3" picks and insert them evenly into the ball. Don't crowd the greens or dried materials too closely. Remember, this is just the foundation. You will add the main accents later to fill in the spaces.

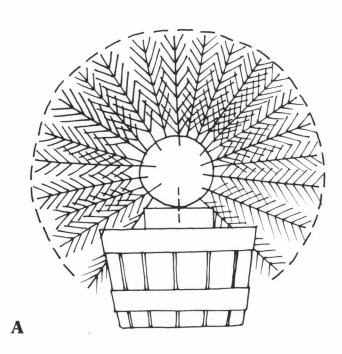

A

HOW TO MAKE A BOW

Bow making is an art in itself. It can be discouraging, since it is not often that success comes after the first try. Be patient. For projects that do require bows and for those of you who do want to make them, here are instructions.

Single Cross Bow for the Christmas Tree and Simple Designs

Take a length of ribbon and place the ribbon as shown (Figure A). Loop a wire through the center, and twist securely in back (Figure B).

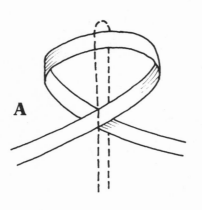

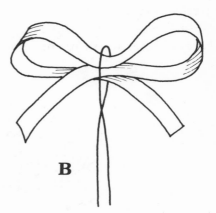

Butterfly Bow

1. Start this bow by forming a circle with the ribbon. Overlap the end (Figure A).

2. With your thumb and forefinger, pinch the ribbon in the center of the circle (Figure B). This is the center of the bow.

3. To make additional loops, hold the center of the bow firmly with your thumb and forefinger.
   - Twist the ribbon below the forefinger (Figure C).
   - Lift up your forefinger.

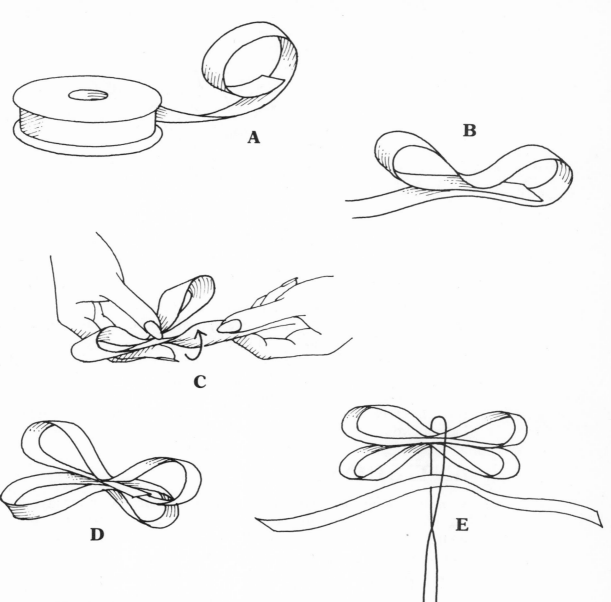

- Quickly slip the twist under the center of the bow.
- Replace the forefinger.
- Make a second loop, slightly larger than the first (Figure D).

Return the ribbon back to the center.

Twist the ribbon again, following the same procedure on the opposite side of the bow.

Add a streamer underneath the center of the ribbon, if desired (Figure E).

Loop a wire through the center, twisting the wire securely in back.

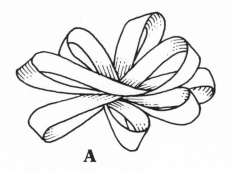

A

The Full Bow

In my opinion, a good bow is not round: an oblong bow creates a more interesting line and more eye appeal. There are only two things to remember when making a full bow.

Always remember to twist your ribbon when you return to the center of the bow.

When you add a loop on the left side, add a loop on the right side. After looping your wire through the center, you can readjust the loops of your bow in any desired position (Figure A).

ANTIQUING

Antiquing means applying a finish to give an object an antique-looking patina. For most items in this book, I used a base coat of flat, white water-base paint or flat oil-base paint. You can use almost any color base to complement your design.

1. Apply one or two coats of base paint, covering the item thoroughly. Allow to dry.

2. Mix one part raw umber oil paint (sold in tubes in any art or craft store) into 3 to 5 parts of flat varnish. The more varnish, the lighter your antiquing stain will be. Mix only the quantity you are going to use.

3. Brush the antiquing solution over the entire base coat.

4. Use cheesecloth or some other soft cloth to wipe away some of the antiquing solution, allowing some of the solution to remain in the crevices of the object. Depending on the degree of "antiquing" you desire, wipe off small or large amounts.

This antiquing method is used by many furniture craftsmen but is not widely known by consumers. Use cheesecloth and burlap to give a smooth or a grainlike appearance respectively. Always leave the edges slightly darker for a more natural antique effect. And don't be afraid to experiment.

If you're unsure about mixing your own antiquing solution, you can purchase white antiquing kits from any paint store, but it costs about three times more than making it yourself.

WHERE TO GET IT FREE —AT THE DUMPS

If you're the kind of person who feels just terrific after you've gotten a bargain—and you're not proud—your local cemetery dump is where it's happening. Styrofoam wreaths in many shapes and sizes, florist picks, and ribbon (all costly if purchased) are available free to those who arrive first at the cemetery dump.

In fact, the awakening of my career began at the depths of the dumps. All the kids in my grammar school were collecting baseball cards, marbles and stamps; I was collecting Styrofoam hearts, wreaths, and other funeral objects. My friends read the comics; I read the obituaries. Through wind, rain, sleet, and snow, I made my daily visit to the cemetery dump.

Every week I brought beautiful, fresh flowers to my grammar school teachers. They were all women who just loved flowers (especially long-stemmed red roses, calla lilies, and birds of paradise). For years, I told them that my grandmother, who lived next door to me in Waterbury, Connecticut, had a big garden.

When I finally decided, just out of grammar school, to make a career and some money at this occupation, I designed in the style that I had learned at the dumps: big—and with lots of color—and people loved it.

Just after I finished high school, my first work appeared in the centerfold of a national magazine. Various companies and organizations asked me to conduct lecture demonstrations and workshop series. As I began spreading the word at these workshops about the discount specials, it was not long before cemetery dumps became the meeting place and social hour of the day for many "crafty" people. Gradually they would rip apart anything that they could get their hands on, and pick it clean. In battling for the bargains, it's each person for him- or herself—and to the quickest go the spoils. I still laugh when I think of one affluent woman, who belittled my activity, disdaining my cemetery dump practices. But obviously she soon re-evaluated the situation. I met her with a full trunk one week later at the dump.

Every cemetery has its own dump. You just have to ride around until you find it or you can discreetly ask the cemetery maintenance personnel. Don't be embarrassed. If you don't get there first, your neighbors might beat you to it.

Color Plate 1   Victorian Blue Centerpiece, page 182

Color Plate 2   Victorian Blue Wreath, page 177

Color Plate 3   Calico Fruit #2, page 43

Color Plate 4   Calico Fruit #1, page 42

Color Plate 5   Gingham Fireside Broom, page 174

Color Plate 6   Paper and Lace: Wreath, page 166; Bouquets, page 171

Color Plate 7   Popcorn and Cranberry Wreath, page 186

Color Plate 8   Country Kitchen, page 87

TWO

A Country Collection

42

CALICO FRUIT BASKET

See also color plates 3 and 4

MATERIALS

Assorted plastic fruit, small and large, enough to fill your basket

Scraps of calico fabric

Wheat paste (sold in paint and wallpaper stores in powder form)

Water (to mix with paste)

1"-diameter Styrofoam balls

Medium wire

Green floral tape

Wicker or rattan basket

Enough Styrofoam pieces to fill your basket

Assorted size florist picks

Artificial greens

2 yards calico ribbon

Single-edge razor (optional)

44

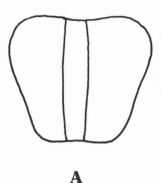

A

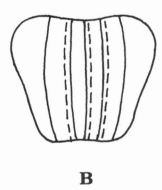

B

1. Cover the larger plastic fruit with the calico fabric. To do this, cut a piece of calico in strips ½″ to ¾″ wide. Mix wheat paste with water to a liquid-paste consistency. Brush the paste sparingly onto the fabric (or use your fingers—it's easier). The paste will come through the front of the fabric. Place the strips vertically on the front of the fruit (Figure A). Smooth out the entire strip so that there are no bumps or ripples. Apply the additional strips by overlapping them slightly at the seam (Figure B). Since most fruit is round or oblong, the fabric strips at the top and bottom will overlap more at the end than in the middle. You need to cover only one half to two thirds of each fruit since only half of the fruit will be exposed in the arrangement. You may have to use smaller pieces of calico to fill in over-rounded or rippled portions of the fruit that will not easily accept a strip of fabric. It is perfectly all right to patch with pieces; when dry, the seams will disappear.

When you have finished covering a piece of fruit, remove all excess wheat paste by patting the fabric with a damp cloth. Remove as much excess paste as possible.

2. To cover the smaller fruit, cut ½″ strips of calico and follow the same procedure as above. You will have to cut up small pieces of fabric to patch the fruit because the fabric is usually too firm to cover the rounded edges neatly.

3. To cover Styrofoam balls, cut a 4″ square from calico and place it over the ball, pulling the four corners together. Twist the fabric tightly in back and wrap securely around the twist. Cover the twist with floral tape.

4. To assemble, fill basket with Styrofoam, right up to the rim. Make a small hole in the back (the uncovered side) of each fruit and insert a 4″ or 6″ florist pick. Put the fruit into the basket, inserting the pick into the Styrofoam, creating a design with the fruit that is complementary to the basket (Figures C-1, C-2, and C-3).

5. Gather cut artificial greens in clusters and place them on assorted size picks. Insert the greens into the spaces between the fruit. Place the wired Styrofoam balls on picks and insert evenly over the entire bouquet. With the calico ribbon, make a butterfly bow with a long, graceful streamer, and place it on the front or top of the basket handle.

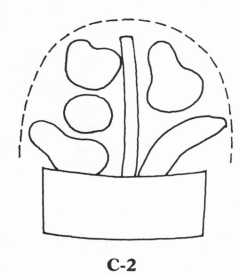

C-2

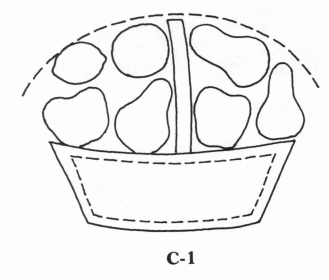

C-1

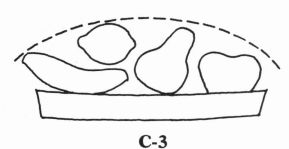

C-3

EGG-CITEMENT

See also color plate 12

MATERIALS

Basket, or wicker or wooden box (approximately 8″ in diameter)
6″-diameter Styrofoam ball
6″-diameter Styrofoam circle (from 1″-thick Styrofoam)
Wheat paste
Water (to mix with paste)
Hay or straw or sphagnum moss
Assorted dried flowers (gypsophila and others)

Calico, gingham, or grosgrain ribbon
2 empty egg cartons (only for real eggs)
30 to 36 white or brown eggs (real or artificial)—at Eastertime it's easy to find good-quality artificial eggs in the flower or garden department of dime stores
Floral glue

For hundreds of years, people removed the white and the yolk from eggshells by simply piercing a hole in both ends of the shell and blowing out the contents. Patiently they sit, blowing each breath as if it were the last, waiting for the last of the white to exude. After making designs with fresh eggs, I had absolutely no doubt whatever that there must be a better way. Therefore, I will first explain the quick, simple artificial-egg procedure, then the tedious, time-consuming, and sloppy procedure using real eggs.

Artificial-Egg Method

1. Most artificial eggs come with their own 3″ plastic pick at the bottom. If yours do not, pierce a hole in the bottom of the egg and insert a 3″ pick.

2. Cut the Styrofoam ball in half. (Since there are two halves, you can easily make two egg centerpieces for the price of one.) Glue the 6″ circle to the bottom of the half ball (Figure A).

3. Starting at the top of the ball, place the eggs, inserting with picks, evenly over the Styrofoam, leaving spaces between the eggs (Figure B). Cover the entire ball with eggs.

4. Mix wheat paste with water until it reaches a semi-fluid consistency. Cut up small pieces of hay in a bowl, adding a little wheat paste at a time, until the mixture becomes a very thick mulch. Put the mixture on the Styrofoam ball between the eggs. When dry, the wheat paste disappears and the hay remains firmly in place.

5. Glue on small pieces of gypsophila (baby's breath) and other dried flowers. Add a butterfly bow if you wish.

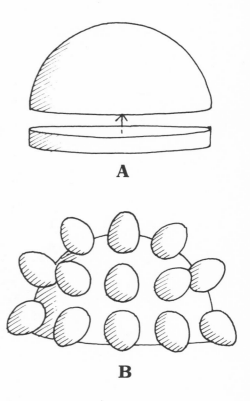

A

B

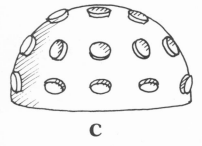

C

Real-Egg Method

1. Pierce tiny holes with a pin at both ends of the eggshell. Blow out the contents.

2. From the empty egg cartons, cut out each of the 12 individual egg holders. Cut each one down, leaving only ½" at the base.

3. Starting at the top of the Styrofoam ball, glue these bases evenly over the entire half sphere, leaving spaces in between (Figure C). When dry, glue the eggs into the cardboard holders.

Follow the same procedure as in artificial eggs for steps 4 and 5.

CALICO RIBBON PLANTER

See also color plate 9

MATERIALS

24" x 12" 1"-thick Styrofoam
Floral glue
Corrugated cardboard (approximately 12" x 6")
2½ yards each of three kinds of 1½"-wide calico ribbons

3 yards dark brown upholstery welting cord (available in fabric stores)
Pipe cleaner
Round toothpicks
Dried materials to fill planter

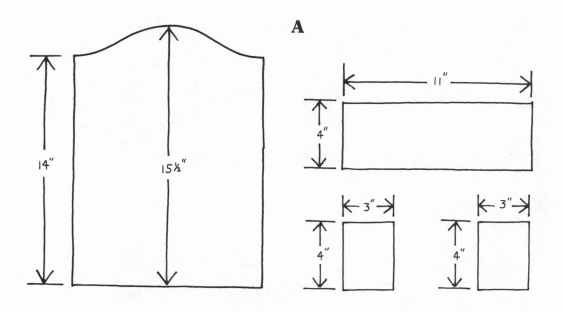

A

14″

15½″

11″

4″

3″

4″

3″

4″

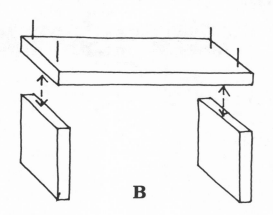

B

50

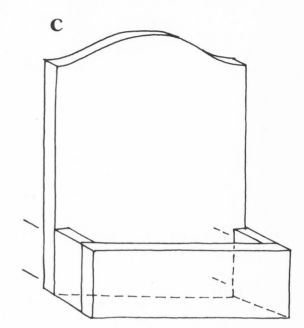

C

1. Cut patterns from Styrofoam (Figure A). To assemble, glue two 3″ x 4″ pieces underneath both ends of the 11″ x 4″ piece (Figure B). Insert toothpicks for additional strength. This is the base of the planter.

2. Glue the base to the front of the 15½″ x 11″ piece. Secure it with toothpicks (Figure C).

3. Cut a 5″ x 11″ piece of corrugated cardboard. Glue the cardboard piece to the bottom of the planter. All the edges of the cardboard should be flush with the edges of the Styrofoam. Trim if necessary.

4. Glue the ribbon to the planter as shown, alternating the three different designs (Figure D). Leave ½″ extra at the top of each ribbon. Next, fold this excess on the top of the planter and glue it in place. You might slit some of these pieces so that they rest smoothly on the top.

5. Apply eight strips of ribbon each about 12″ long vertically to the bottom of the cardboard base. Overlap a ½″ seam from the front to the back of the planter.

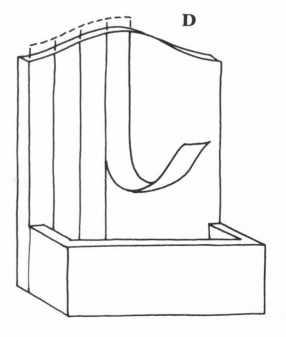

D

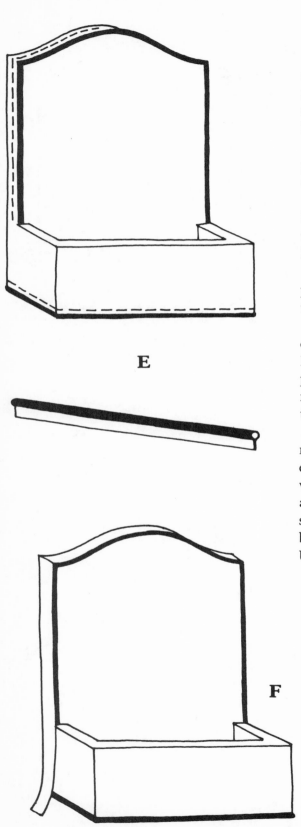

E

F

6. Glue welting cord around the seams (Figure E). Place the seam of the welting cord inward, allowing the cording to overlap the edge of the Styrofoam slightly, creating a bevel. Make sure to square the corners neatly.

7. Glue the ribbon to the side of the planter, covering the seam of the welting cord. Fold the excess ribbon over to the back.

8. Glue three strips of ribbon about 20″ long horizontally around the entire front of the planter, leaving ½″ extra on both ends. Fold and glue the excess to the back.

9. Glue the welting cord on the back of the planter, laying the seam along the edges of the Styrofoam (Figure F).

10. To hang, make a loop with the pipe cleaner and glue to the back of the planter. Place a block of Styrofoam or Sahara into the planter. Fill with your choice of dried materials. Be sure that the colors are complementary to your ribbon.

Note: You can cover this planter with fabric, wallpaper, or cork. And you can change it easily. When you change draperies or wallpaper simply remove the ribbon and apply the new covering. Tin cans, canister sets, picture frame mats, and bottles can also be covered with the same fabric or wallpaper. Use them as a decorative accent.

TONGUE DEPRESSOR PLANTER

See also color plate 11

MATERIALS

Tongue depressors (available in most drugstores or from your friendly physician, who might even give them to you free). As a substitute, use thin wood slats from old wooden porch blinds, or any kind of wooden stick, even popsicle sticks.

Assorted dried materials and/or shells to fill planter

21" x 12" 1"-thick white Styrofoam

Hacksaw

White glue

Round toothpicks

Corrugated cardboard at least 12" × 6"

Straight pins (optional)

Good cutting shears or paper cutter

Medium-size upholstery tacks

Shellac or primer sealer

2 oil stains: ⅛ light and 1 fairly dark

Varnish (optional)

Sahara or Oasis

Pipe cleaner

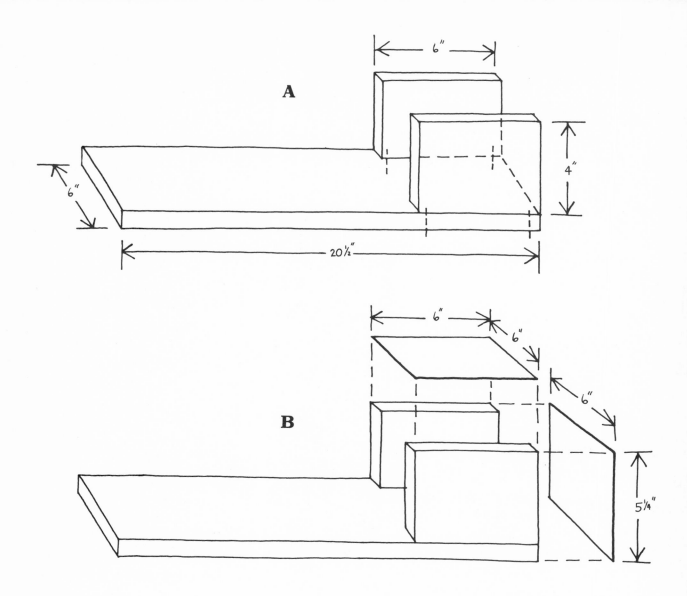

A

6"

4"

6"

20½"

B

6"

6"

6"

5¼"

Note: Remember that the width of your planter (approximately 6") will vary slightly, depending on the width of your tongue depressors or wooden slats. No extra cutting or piecing is necessary if you make the width of your planter a multiple of the width of your tongue depressors or slats. For example, the strips I used were ⅞" wide. Multiplied by seven strips across the width equaled 6⅛″. Do the same with your strips, then adjust the width of your planter. Some of the other measurements will vary slightly with your dimensions.

1. From the Styrofoam sheet, cut a 20½″ x 6″ piece and two 4″ x 6″ pieces. Use a hacksaw blade, but be sure that you cut slowly and carefully so that the edges are smooth and even.

2. Place the two 4″ x 6″ pieces on top of the larger piece, and glue in place (Figure A). This is the base of the planter. Insert round toothpicks from the back of the planter into the sides for extra support.

3. From the corrugated cardboard, cut two pieces, one 6″ x 6″ and one 5¼″ x 6″. Glue the 6″ x 6″ piece to the front across the two pieces of Styrofoam (Figure B). Glue the remaining cardboard piece to the bottom. You can insert straight pins through the cardboard into the Styrofoam to hold them together firmly in place until dry.

4. Cut assorted lengths from your tongue depressors or wooden slats, approximately 3″ to 4″. Use good cutting shears or, better yet, a paper cutter. Be sure that both ends of strips are straight; otherwise, your "parquet" will not fit together neatly on the Styrofoam.

5. Starting at the top of the planter, glue strips to the Styrofoam one at a time. Be sure that you butt the edges together firmly (Figure C). Remove any excess glue as you go along or it will show when you apply the stain.

6. When the top is completely dry, follow the same procedure for the sides and the bottom of the planter.

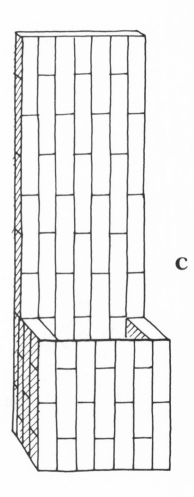

C

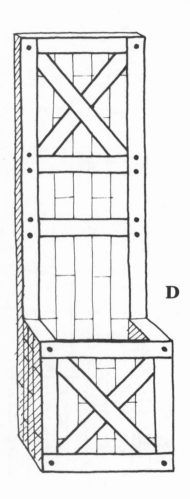

D

7. When the entire planter is dry, cut additional strips and apply them over the tongue depressors (Figure D). When these strips have dried thoroughly, you can insert upholstery tacks at the intersections.

8. Apply one coat of shellac or primer sealer to the entire planter. Let it dry thoroughly. Paint one coat of the lighter oil stain over the entire planter. Let it completely dry. Next, apply some of the darker stain, using a firm brush. Remove the excess by rubbing the brush onto the newspaper until it is almost dry. "Dry brush" the surface lightly to achieve a slight color contrast which will create an antique patina. If you desire a very realistic patina, use the antiquing solution in Chapter 1 instead of the darker stain.

9. Apply a coat of varnish if you wish. Insert a piece of Sahara or Oasis into the base of the planter. Fill with your choice of dried materials, cloth, or silk flowers.

10. To make a hanging planter, form a loop with a pipe cleaner. Glue the ends, 3″ apart, to the back of the base.

PLANTER VARIATION

MATERIALS

This project requires the same materials as the preceding "Tongue Depressor Planter."

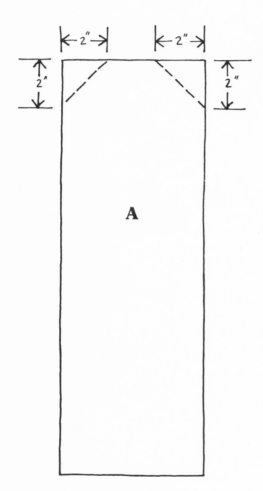

Note: Remember that the width of your planter (approximately 6″) will vary slightly, depending on the width of your tongue depressors or wooden slats. No extra cutting or piecing is necessary if you make the width of your planter a multiple of the width of your tongue depressors or slats. For example, the strips I used were ⅞″ wide. Multiplied by seven strips across, the width equaled 6⅛″. Do the same with your strips, then adjust the width of your planter. Some of the other measurements will vary slightly with your dimensions.

1. From the Styrofoam sheet, cut an 18″ x 6″ piece. Use a hacksaw blade. Be sure that you cut slowly and carefully so that the edges are smooth and even. At one end, measure 2″ inward and 2″ down from the corners. Make a dotted line and cut neatly along it (Figure A).

2. Reproduce the second pattern onto the Styrofoam (Figure B). Make two of them and cut neatly with the hacksaw. Glue these pieces on top of the 18″ x 6″ piece in place (Figure C). This is the base of the planter. Insert round toothpicks from the back of the planter and into the sides for extra support.

3. Cut two pieces from the corrugated cardboard: 6″ x 3″ (the front) and 6″ x 4¾″ (the bottom). Glue the 6″ x 3″ piece to the front across the two pieces of Styrofoam

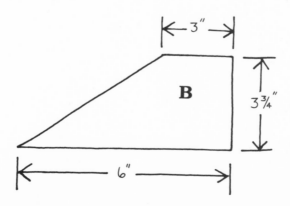

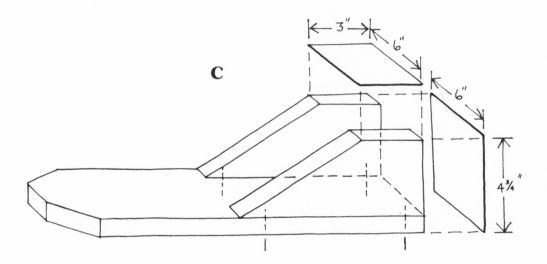

C

3″   6″   6″

4¾″

(Figure C). Glue the remaining piece to the bottom. You can insert straight pins through the cardboard into the Styrofoam to hold them firmly in place until dry.

4. Next, cut assorted lengths from tongue depressors or wooden slats, approximately 3″ to 4″. Use good cutting shears or a paper cutter. Be sure that both ends of slats are straight or your "parquet" will not fit together neatly on the Styrofoam.

5. Starting at the top of the planter, glue on strips one at a time. In order to cut the corners at the top neatly and evenly, place the depressor in the exact position. With a sharp pencil, inscribe a line along the back of the Styrofoam edge (Figure D). Cut neatly on the line. As you apply each strip,

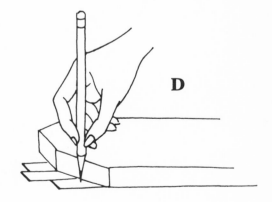

D

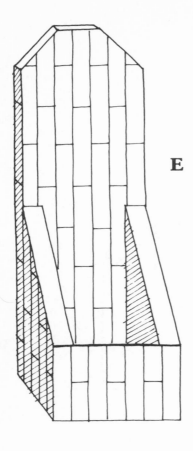

E

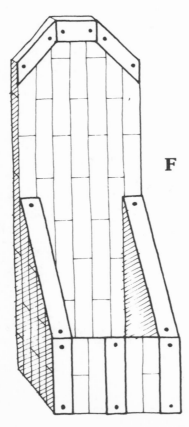

F

be sure that the edges touch (Figure E). Remove any excess glue as you go along or it will show when you apply the stain.

6. When the top is completely dry, follow the same procedure for the sides and the bottom of the planter. You might have to inscribe a line with a pencil at the angles along the sides.

7. When the planter is entirely dry, glue additional strips over the tongue depressors (Figure F). When these strips have dried you can insert upholstery tacks at the intersections.

8. Apply one coat of shellac or primer sealer to the entire planter. Let it dry. Place one coat of the lighter oil stain over the entire planter. Let that dry thoroughly. Then, place some of the darker stain on a firm brush. Remove the excess by applying the brush to newspaper until the brush is almost dry. "Dry brush" lightly over the entire surface of the planter, giving variation to create an artificial patina. You may also wish to spatter some of the stain lightly on the wood for a weathered effect.

9. Insert a piece of Sahara or Oasis in the planter. Fill with your choice shells, dried materials and/or silk or cloth flowers. *Note:* If you are using shells, it is easy to wire them. Simply glue a small piece of Styrofoam to the back of each shell (or into any shell cavities). Then glue a heavy wire into the Styrofoam. Place the wired shells on picks.

10. To make a hanging planter, form a loop with a pipe cleaner. Glue the ends, 3" apart, to the back of the base.

GYPSOPHILA WREATH

See also color plate 13

MATERIALS

German statice

14"-diameter white Styrofoam wreath

Dried gypsophila (baby's breath)

White floral tape

Straight pins

White floral buttons (available where dried materials are sold)

Medium and fine wire

2 yards ⅜"-wide cream colored velvet ribbon

Floral glue

3" florist picks

3 yards 1½"-wide cream colored velvet ribbon

Masking tape

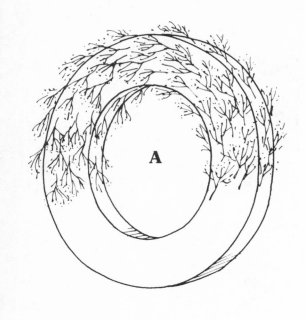

A

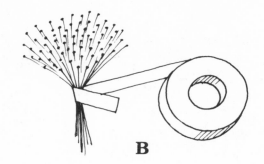

B

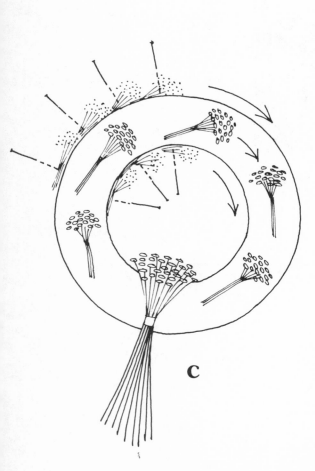

C

1. Cut 3″ to 4″ long pieces of statice. Starting on the side of the wreath and going in one direction, insert statice stems directly into the wreath. Keep statice fairly close to the wreath frame. Continue to cover the top and inside of the frame with statice (Figure A).

2. Make small clusters of dried gypsophila (baby's breath), approximately 4″ long (Figure B). Bunch the stems together and cover them firmly with floral tape.

3. Place the clusters one at a time on the side of the wreath in the following manner. Going in one direction, place a straight pin into the taped stem of each cluster (Figure C). As you go along, overlap the preceding stems with the following cluster. Continue this procedure all around the edge of the wreath.

4. Follow the same procedure for the inside and top of the wreath, creating as even a shape as possible. For additional height and roundness, place the clusters on the top of the wreath on 3″ picks, and insert them into the Styrofoam.

5. Make a 14″-long cluster of floral buttons with the stems suspended. Wrap a wire around the stems approximately one fourth of the way down. Insert the wired buttons into the center of the Styrofoam (Figure C).

Make five smaller clusters, approximately 4″ long, of floral buttons with stems suspended. Wrap a wire around the center of each cluster. Twist the wire securely in back.

6. Cut five 12″ lengths of ⅜″ ribbon. Starting 5″ from the edge of the ribbon, wrap the ribbon diagonally around the stems (Figure D). There should be two diagonal wraps. Cover the exposed wire with one of the wraps. Place a little glue at the beginning and at the end of the two wraps.

7. Place the wired clusters on 3″ picks and insert as shown in Figure C. Weave the excess ribbon streamers throughout the gypsophila. Use a small amount of glue to hold the extended streamers in place.

8. To make the bow, cut nine 8″ lengths of 1½″ velvet ribbon. Since the velvet ribbon is too limp to hold a firm bow, it helps to use masking tape and wire for body. Place the wire down the middle of the adhesive side of the tape (Figure E). Cut nine 9″ strips of wired tape. Place the wired tape on the back of the ribbon. Form a loop with each strip and place the ends on a 3″ pick (Figure F). Make an oval around the large cluster of floral buttons. Place the additional loops in the center of the oval. Cut the remaining ribbon in half. Place them on 3″ picks, and insert as streamers below the ribbon.

63

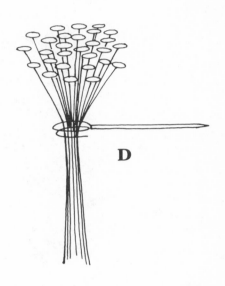

D

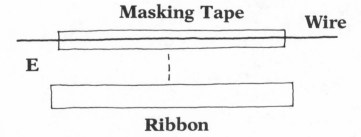

Masking Tape **Wire**

E

Ribbon

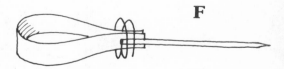

F

TEASEL BOUQUET

MATERIALS

Compass
4" x 4" block 2"-thick Styrofoam
Hacksaw
6"-long pipe cleaner
Sphagnum moss
Floral glue
10 natural-colored teasels
3" wire picks

German statice
Dried gypsophila (baby's breath)
19 natural-colored wheat
White floral tape
Heavy wire
14 1"-diameter Styrofoam balls
3 yards 2"-wide plaid ribbon or fabric

1. Using a compass, round off one side of the 4" x 4" Styrofoam block. Cut the arc carefully with a hacksaw. For hanging, glue the two ends of a 6" pipe cleaner 3" apart, forming a loop, into the top back of the arc. Glue sphagnum moss over the top and sides of the Styrofoam.

2. Cut the ten teasels leaving 2" stems. Save the stems from the teasels for use later. Place nine of the cut teasels on 3" picks, halfway up the teasel stem.

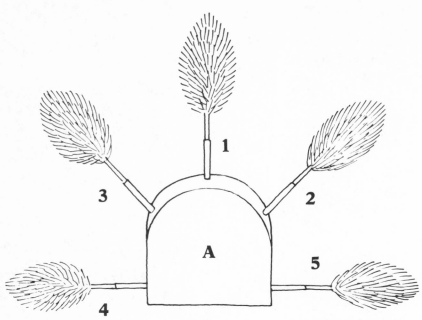

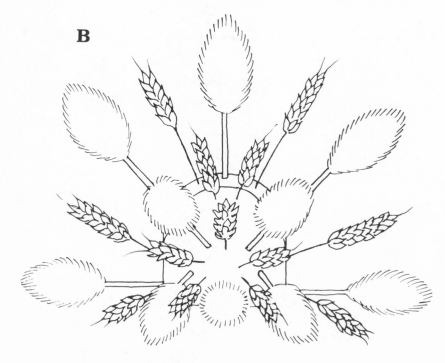

3. Insert teasels numbers 1 through 5 into the sides of the block as shown in Figure A. Insert teasels number 6 through 9 into the center of the block. Space them evenly as shown, slightly outward from the Styrofoam, creating a mounded effect (Figure B). This mound creates depth, eliminating the possibility of a flat-looking bouquet. Leave a space near the bottom for the remaining single teasel to be inserted later.

4. Cut pieces of statice and insert the stems directly into the Styrofoam. Cover it evenly with statice. The statice serves to cover the Styrofoam and at the same time provides body for the gypsophila (baby's breath).

5. Make small, airy clusters of gypsophila and place on 3″ picks. Cover with floral tape. Insert the gypsophila between the statice until the bouquet is adequately filled.

6. Cut short pieces of wheat, saving the stems. Place the wheat on picks and insert into the bouquet (Figure B).

7. Glue two thirds of the wheat stems and all of the teasel stems into the bottom of the Styrofoam (Figure C). Arrange the stems in a small fanlike design, some extending upward and outward.

8. Place the remaining teasel on a 7″ length of heavy wire. Secure the teasel to the wire with floral tape. Place the wired teasel, facing upward and almost directly outward, into the space at the bottom. The

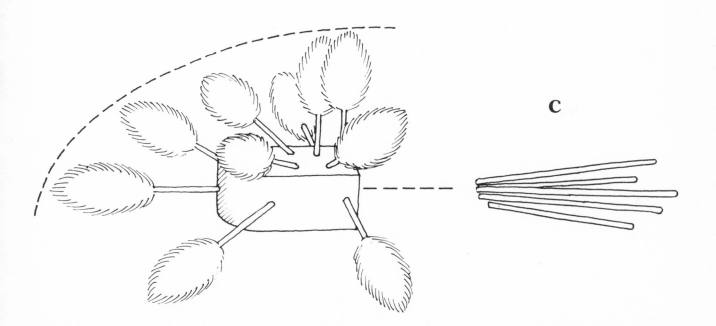

C

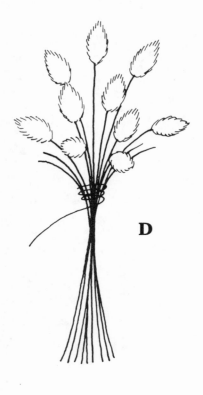

D

wire stem enables you to angle the teasel in any position. Bring the wire down to the stems below. Wrap a thin wire around the entire cluster of stems to hold the teasel in place (Figure D).

9. Place the remaining one third of the wheat stems in the lower part of the bouquet, so that the stems appear to be coming from the dried materials. Gather the wheat stems around the cluster of stationary stems. Wrap a thin wire around the entire cluster of stems.

10. Next, cover the Styrofoam balls by putting glue over half of each ball. Then place a piece of ribbon over each one stretching the ribbon tightly. Smooth out as many wrinkles and bumps as possible and cut off the excess neatly. Only half the ball will show in the bouquet. Or you can cover the balls with fabric (the easier way) by cutting a 4″ square (Figure E-1). Place the fabric over the ball, pulling the four corners together. Twist the fabric tightly in back (Figure E-2). Wrap a wire around the twist and cover with floral tape (Figure E-3).

11. Glue the completed balls directly to the gypsophila.

12. Make a full bow with streamers, and wire it around the stems.

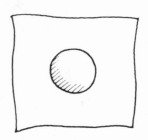

E-1

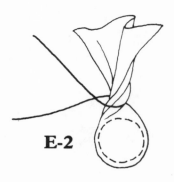

E-2

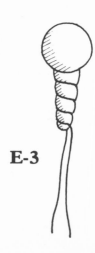

E-3

OLD SACK WITH A NEW BAG

See also color plate 15

MATERIALS

12″ circle of natural, cream, or bright-colored burlap purchased or cut from old potato sacks. (Go to any local vegetable wholesaler or retailer, who will probably be happy to give the potato sacks to you.)

Small pieces of Sahara or Oasis
Sand or fine gravel
Natural string or jute
German statice
Sphagnum moss
Assorted dried materials
Compass

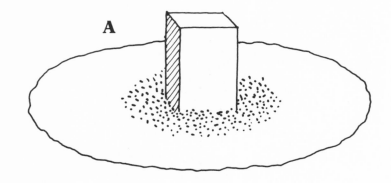

A

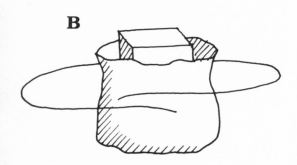

B

C

Note: This project is mistake-proof. It is quick and inexpensive, and no matter what you do, it comes out looking absolutely terrific. Great for last-minute gifts and bazaars.

1. Cut a circle 12″ in diameter from burlap. (Actually, you can use almost any size circle, but the bigger the circle, the larger the sack will be, and the more dried materials required.)

2. Cut a 2½″ x 2¼″ x 4″ block of Sahara. Stand it vertically in the center of the circle. Place fine sand or gravel around the base of the Sahara (Figure A). This will weigh down the bottom of the sack and also fill it out.

3. Bring all the ends of the circle together up to the Sahara, creating the sack (Figure B). Wrap a string of jute around the burlap, three fourths of the way up, and knot it securely (Figure C). Reshape the base of the sack if necessary. *Variation:* To make a firmer, more permanent, and more stylized sack, place the burlap circle in wheat paste mixed to a semifluid consistency. Remove the burlap and place it on wax paper. Place a drinking glass in the center of the circle. Bring all the ends of the circle

together around the glass. Tie a string around the burlap, three fourths of the way up. Shape the bottom of the sack, if you desire. When dry, the sack becomes hard and firm. You can varnish it for a glossy effect, if you like.

4. Fill your sack with statice. Insert the stems directly into the Sahara. Almost any design you choose will work well (Figures D-1, D-2, and D-3).

5. When the basic shape is complete, add your main flowers. These are usually larger or spiky. Once you have created your basic design with these, add the remaining fillers or smaller flowers. You can also use silk or cloth flowers along with the dried materials. At Christmas, you can use red or green burlap for the sack and fill it with pine and assorted holiday trims.

Note: If you want to make a sack with a really fine, delicate flower arrangement, cover the exposed Sahara with sphagnum moss. This will allow you to create designs as feathery as you wish without having the stems or the Sahara show.

D-1

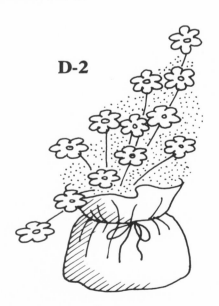

D-2

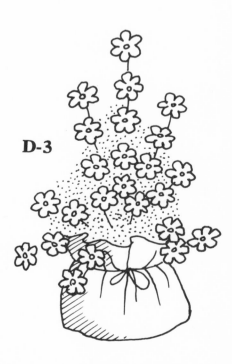

D-3

WITCH'S BROOM WREATH

MATERIALS

12"-diameter half-rounded Styro-
   foam wreath
Witch's broom, dried stems or
   branches or any local dried
   reed or grass that will bend
Brown tape
Small hand or electric drill
Peach pits

Medium wire
Eastern white pinecones
Bleach
Spray varnish or shellac
Acorns
White glue
Assorted dried materials
3" florist picks

1. To make the wreath, cover the Styrofoam wreath with one cut-up layer of witch's broom, dried stems, or wild grass. Wrap wire around the grass to hold it to the wreath. This is done simply to cover the exposed Styrofoam. Cut pieces of grass, 10″ to 12″ in length. Group one cluster of the grass onto the top and sides of the wreath (Figure A). Wrap tape at the base of the stems around the wreath. Going in one direction, follow the same procedure overlapping the taped stems with the following cluster. The effect that should be achieved when complete is a wispy, circular movement. Almost all natural grasses will bend gracefully with a little help.

2. Drill a small hole into the base of each peach pit. Loop a wire through the hole and twist securely below. Make 11 to 17 flowerettes from Eastern white pinecones. After you have wired the flowerettes and the peach pits, place them in full strength bleach for 3 to 10 minutes. When dry, spray them with one or two coats of spray varnish or shellac.

3. Drill two holes, ½″ apart, into the base of the empty acorn shells. Loop a wire through the holes and twist the wire firmly below. Glue the acorns into the shells.

4. Place the wired flowerettes on 3″ picks and insert them into the Styrofoam, in a semi-crescent design. Fill in between the spaces with the wired peach pits and acorns. Place any additional dried flowers which you wish to use as a color accent on 3″ picks and place evenly among the flowerettes and the seeds. You may also use a bow if you wish.

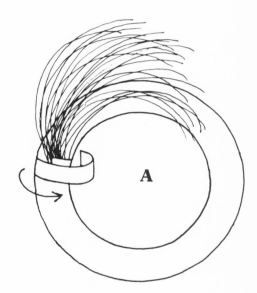

A

COUNTRY JARS

MATERIALS

Here's a quick accessory to complement any project. All you need is glue, assorted widths of calico, velvet, cotton, or eyelet ribbons or trim, and old or new jars. Use any combination of ribbons and glue them to the jars, covering as much or as little of the surfaces as you like.

Color Plate 9   Calico Ribbon Planter, page 49

Color Plate 10   Hearth Basket, page 93

Color Plate 11   Tongue Depressor Planter #1, page 53

Color Plate 12   Egg-Citement, page 46

Color Plate 13   Gypsophila Wreath, page 61

Color Plate 14   Basket of Flowerettes, page 90

Color Plate 15   Old Sack with a New Bag, page 69

Color Plate 16   Peach Pit Special, page 84

THREE

Nature's Own

PEACH PIT SPECIAL

See also color plate 16

MATERIALS

Peach pits (at least 25)
Household bleach
Acorns (at least 25)
Medium wire
Electric or hand drill
White glue
Half a basket or a wall planter
Styrofoam block to fit container
German statice or sphagnum
  moss

Florist picks, assorted sizes
Dried gypsophila (baby's breath)
Floral glue
Tiny dried flowers to go with
  your color design
Cornhusk, 1½″ wide
Masking tape
Gloss varnish
Stapler
Wheat or any dried grass

1. Place peach pits in full-strength bleach. When you obtain the desired lightness, remove the pits and allow them to dry. Drill a small hole through the base of each peach pit.

2. Insert a wire through each hole. Bring the wire down and twist securely. If you do the wiring correctly, each shell or cone should remain upright when you hold the end of the wire. The correct tension to the twist of the wire eliminates drooping as you create your design. Dip the pits into varnish, or spray them with varnish.

3. Drill two holes, approximately ¼" apart, into the bottom of the empty acorns. Using an 8" length of wire, loop it through the two holes from the top of the shell (Figure A). Twist the ends of the wire securely below. Glue the acorn into the empty shell with white glue. Dip the acorns into varnish, or spray them with varnish.

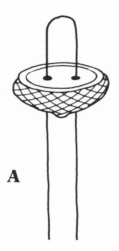

A

4. Bleach the half basket or rattan wall planter in household bleach, if you wish. When dry, place the Styrofoam block tightly into the container.

5. Starting at the top of the basket and working your way downward, place the peach pits on assorted-size florist picks, and insert them sparsely, creating the basic outline and design for your bouquet (Figure B). This design should complement the lines of your container. Once you achieve the desired outline, fill in with the remaining peach pits and acorns.

6. Fill the spaces in between the acorns and peach pits with either statice or sphagnum moss. Sphagnum moss is quicker since

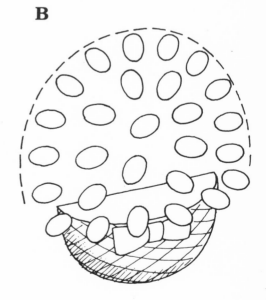

B

all you have to do is stuff the moss in between the spaces. If you use statice, insert the stems directly into the Styrofoam. Do not pack it tightly.

7. Glue small clusters of gypsophila (baby's breath) to the statice or the sphagnum moss, using floral glue. Glue dried wheat or grass or any additional dried flowers that you may wish to use as a color accent.

8. For the ribbon, cut two 8″ strips of cornhusk. Place a wire centrally down the adhesive side of the masking tape, and place the tape on the back of the cornhusk strips. From another cornhusk, cut a 4″ strip. Wire as above.

9. To assemble the bow, form a loop with each 8″ cornhusk segment. Place the two ends, overlapping each other, to create a bow. Staple securely together. Loop the 4″ strip around the center of the bow (Figure C). Staple securely to the back of the bow. Cut two streamers and wire the ends together. Wrap a wire through the center of the bow and place it on a florist pick. Insert the bow wherever you wish.

C

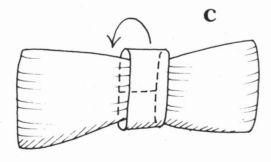

COUNTRY KITCHEN

See also color plate 8

MATERIALS

4″ x 6″ block 1″-thick white Styrofoam

16″-diameter round rattan tray or mat or flat woven basket

Thin wire

4 white chenille stems

3 fresh bagels

3″ florist picks

13 breadsticks

German statice

Dried gypsophila (baby's breath)

Brown or white floral tape

Thin pretzel sticks

Electric or hand drill

Stiff heavy wire

Popcorn (one pot or popper)

Medium wire

Walnuts

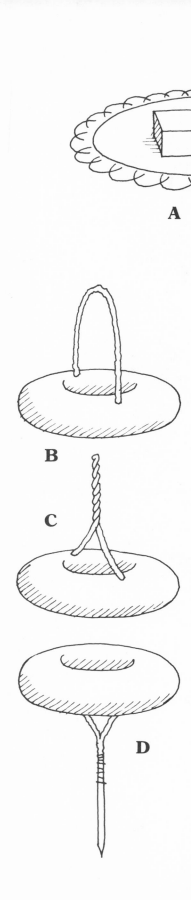

A

B

C

D

1. Place the Styrofoam block in the center of the rattan tray. Loop a wire through the block to the back of the tray (Figure A). Twist the ends of the wire in back to hold the Styrofoam block securely in place.

2. Cut two white chenille stems in half. Glue the two ends of a 6″ chenille stem to the back of each fresh bagel on either side of the hole, forming a loop (Figure B). Twist the center of the loop until there is no slack (Figure C).

3. Place the twisted chenille stem on a 3″ pick (Figure D). Insert the three bagels into the Styrofoam (Figure E).

4. Divide nine breadsticks in groups of three. Wrap three breadsticks together with a 6″ chenille piece around the middle of the breadsticks. Very carefully twist the stem in back so that the breadsticks won't break.

5. Cut pieces of statice and insert the stems directly into the Styrofoam block. Cover the block evenly with the statice, leaving a border of approximately 2½″ wide on either side of the rattan tray.

6. Place the three clusters of breadsticks on 3″ picks, and insert into Styrofoam as shown.

7. Make small clusters of dried gypsophila (baby's breath) and place on 3″ picks. Insert the clusters over the statice so that the bouquet appears to be made entirely from gypsophila.

8. Very carefully break the remaining breadsticks in half. Place each half, broken side down, carefully on a 3″ pick. Cover the wired part of the pick with floral tape. Follow the same procedure for the thin whole pretzel sticks.

9. Neatly crack the walnut shells in half, keeping the shells intact. Remove the nutmeats. Drill a small hole at the base of each shell. Loop a wire through each shell and bring the wire down, twisting it securely. Place the wired shells on 3″ picks. Insert the breadsticks, pretzels, and walnut shells evenly in the Styrofoam throughout the design.

10. Cut 4″ to 6″ pieces of stiff heavy wire. Glue one wire to the center of each popcorn. Insert the wired popcorn in any empty spaces that remain in the design.

11. To make the bow loops, string popcorn through three 8″ lengths of medium wire. Leave a small space at both ends of the wire. Form a loop with each 8″ piece. Twist the two ends of the wire together and cover the wire with floral tape.

12. With a needle and thread, string two popcorn streamers, one 11″ and one 17″ long. Fasten the ends of the streamers to the wired bow. Place the completed bow on a 3″ pick and insert into the Styrofoam at the bottom of the design.

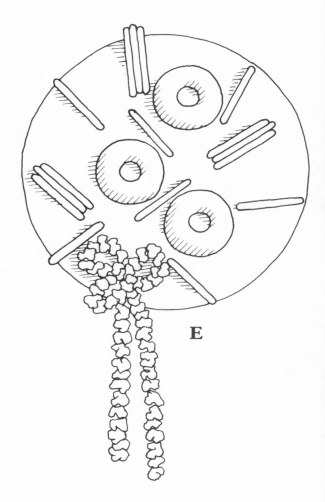

E

BASKET OF FLOWERETTES

See also color plate 14

MATERIALS

4½" square strawberry basket, or any 4" to 5" square container	White floral buttons
Eastern white pinecones	6"-diameter Styrofoam ball
Medium wire	Sphagnum moss
Household bleach	Dried gypsophila (baby's breath)
Gloss varnish	1½ yards 1½"-wide dotted swiss, polka dot, or other cotton ribbon
15 brown chenille stems	
Floral glue	Hat pins

90

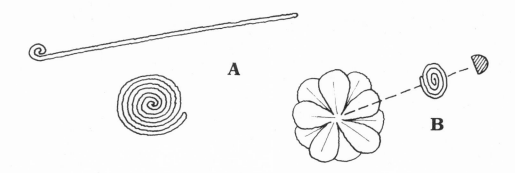

A

B

1. Make 40 to 50 pinecone flowerettes. In order to create an even mound shape, all the flowerettes should have a uniform depth of three to four layers of petals.

2. Wire each flowerette. Place all the pinecones in bleach. After bleaching to desired lightness, allow them to dry. The cones should open fully when dry.

3. Dip the flowerettes into gloss varnish. Allow the excess to drip off. When the cones are completely dry, apply another coat of varnish. You could also use spray varnish, which is much quicker, but you will have to apply more coats to achieve a thick high-gloss finish.

4. To make the center of the flowerette, cut a 3″ to 4″ length of brown chenille stem. Starting from one end, roll each piece into a tight coil (Figure A). Glue a floral button in the center of the coil (Figure B). The chenille coil should be larger than the floral button. Glue the entire coil to the center of the varnished flowerette.

5. To assemble, place enough Styrofoam into the strawberry basket so that two thirds of the ball remains above the rim of

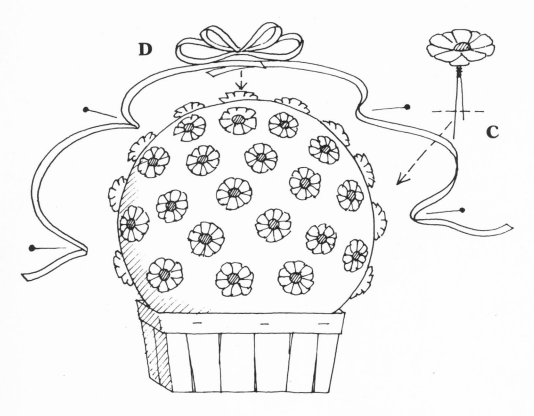

the basket. Cut the wire on each flowerette to 2″ long (Figure C). Place a small amount of glue on each wire and insert each flowerette evenly over two thirds of the Styrofoam ball. Leave spaces between the flowerettes.

6. Fill in between the spaces of the flowerettes with sphagnum moss. Glue it firmly in place.

7. Glue small pieces of gypsophila (baby's breath) to the statice. Make additional coils of chenille stems and floral buttons and glue them to the gyp between the flowerettes' spaces.

8. Make a butterfly with the ribbon, using the excess ribbon as the streamer. Place the bow on top of the bouquet (Figure D) and weave the streamers gracefully over the bouquet. Secure each loop to the Styrofoam ball with hat pins.

HEARTH BASKET

See also color plate 10

MATERIALS

2″-thick white Styrofoam, the size of your basket

Rattan or wicker fruit basket, with a handle, if possible

2 or more small blocks of 2″ thick Styrofoam

Assorted varieties, shapes, and sizes pinecones

Gloss spray varnish

Floral glue

Household bleach

Heavy medium wire

4″, 6″, and 8″ florist picks

German statice

Dried gypsophila (baby's breath)

1½ yards 1½″-wide brown velvet ribbon and/or cornhusk ribbon

Wheat

1. Place the largest Styrofoam block securely into the bottom of the basket. The depth of the basket and the height you want your bouquet to be determine how many additional blocks one on top of the other to create a pyramid effect (Figure A). The Styrofoam should be approximately half as high as the basket.

2. To fill the basket, use as many different varieties, shapes, and sizes of pinecones as you can. Incorporate the fronts, sides, backs, and flowerettes for interesting texture. Put some of the flowerettes in bleach to lighten some cones to give color variation or shading to your wreath.

3. Wrap medium or heavy wire around the base of each cone. The gauge you use depends on the weight of the pinecones. Heavy wire also keeps the pinecones upright and securely in place after they are inserted into the design.

4. Place the wired cones on assorted-size florist picks. Starting at the top of your basket and working your way down, insert long spike cones into the Styrofoam, creating the basic outline for your bouquet (Figure B). Once you achieve the desired shape, fill in with the remaining cones. Place the larger cones at the bottom so that the arrangement does not look top-heavy. Leave spaces between the cones. Spray with one or two coats of varnish.

5. Place clusters of statice on picks and insert between pinecone spaces. If you are on a tight budget, you may fill the spaces with swamp grass or other dried grasses that you gather. The statice (or dried grass) need not extend outward from the cones, since its main purpose is to provide body

and hold the entire design more firmly together.

6. Glue small clusters of gyp (baby's breath) to the statice or dried material, so that the arrangement appears to be made entirely of gyp. You can also place larger clusters of gyp on assorted-size florist picks and insert them evenly over the statice. This method requires more gyp than gluing the clusters.

7. Place the wheat on assorted-size florist picks and insert them evenly throughout the bouquet. Add a velvet bow (or any other kind that you desire) at the top of the handle or the bouquet.

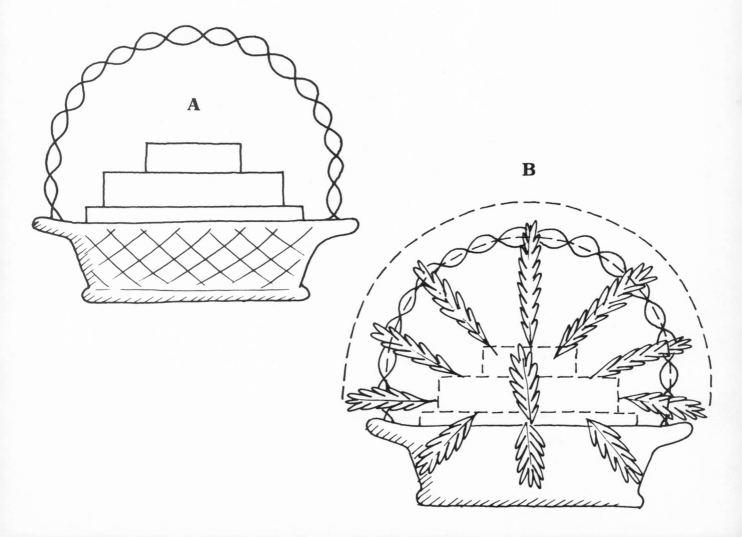

PHEASANT AND PODS

MATERIALS

15 pheasant tail feathers
3″ florist picks
6″ x 4″ sheet 1″-thick Styrofoam
5 brown lotus pods
Germane statice
3 yards 1½″-wide brown velvet ribbon
3 yards 2½″-wide cornhusk, burlap, or ribbon with a natural or wheat color

Dried gypsophila (baby's breath)
Medium wire
Floral glue
Tree bark (optional). You can purchase tree bark from a nursery or lumber store. If you want to be adventurous, hunt in the woods for decayed or dead trees from which the bark can be easily removed.

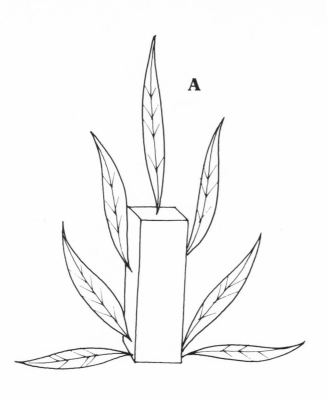

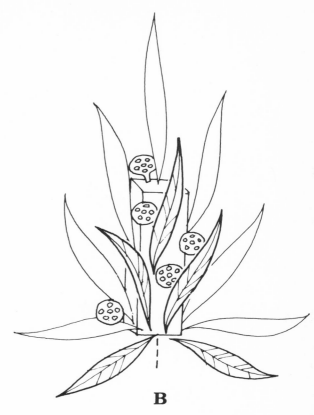

1. Place 12 tail feathers on 3″ picks. Starting at the top of the Styrofoam sheet, insert seven feathers as shown (Figure A). Place the feathers as parallel as possible to the block. The next five feathers in the center should extend outward from the block (Figure B). This gives the depth and fullness.

2. Place the five lotus pods on picks and insert between the feathers as shown in Figure B.

3. Cut pieces of statice and insert the stems directly into the Styrofoam. Place the statice between the feathers, covering most of the exposed surface.

4. Make airy clusters of gyp (baby's breath) and place on 3″ picks until you feel the design is adequately filled. You could incorporate additional dried materials as color accents.

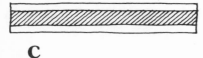

C

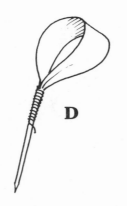

D

5. To make the bow, glue the velvet ribbon lengthwise down the center of the cornhusk ribbon (Figure C).

6. Cut five 10″ strips of the double ribbon. Make a single loop with each strip by pinching the end of each strip together and fastening it to a 3″ pick (Figure D).

7. Place the five loops into the Styrofoam bottom below the feathers, creating a bow. Cut two ribbon streamers, one 20″ and one 15″ in length. Place these on picks and insert them below the five loops (Figure E).

8. Wire the three remaining feathers together and secure them to the center of the bow with wire (Figure E). Place the entire design on a piece of tree bark if you wish. Secure the entire design to the bark by looping wire around the Styrofoam, then into the back of the bark. Twist the wire securely.

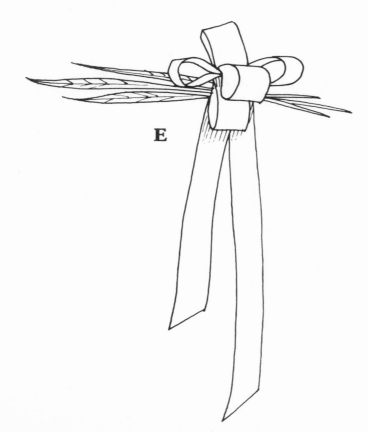

E

PINECONE TREE

See also color plate 23

MATERIALS

2 sheets 13″ square corrugated
   cardboard or 1 sheet thin plywood
Glue
12″-diameter bushel or basket
Medium-mesh chicken wire
Stapler

Cutting pliers
Assorted varieties, shapes, and
   sizes pinecones
Spray gloss varnish
Dried gypsophila (baby's breath)
   and wheat
1 yard brown velvet ribbon

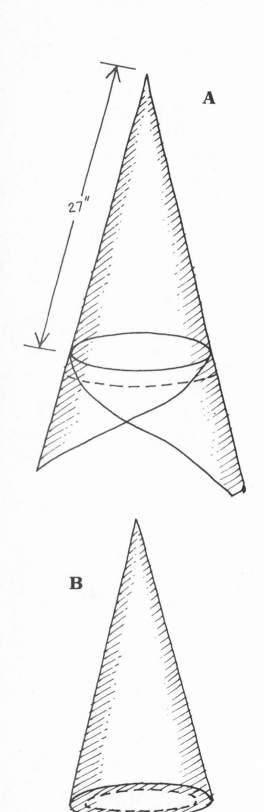

A

27″

B

1. From corrugated cardboard, cut two circles, slightly wider than 12″ in diameter. (They should be slightly larger then the rim of your bushel or container). Glue the two cardboard circles together for strength. If you want even more strength, use plywood as the base instead of cardboard.

2. Using the circle as the base of the tree form, mold a cone shape with the chicken wire around the cardboard disk (Figure A). Form as even a tree cone as possible. Make it approximately 27″ high. Cut off the excess chicken wire with cutting pliers.

3. Weave the ends of the chicken wire together, keeping the cone shape intact. Cut off the excess wire below the bottom of the cardboard, leaving 1½″ margin below (Figure B). Bend and fold this excess under the circle and staple securely in place.

3. Using 10 to 12 different kinds and sizes of pinecones, incorporate the front, back, and flowerettes of pinecones. Soak all the cones in water and allow them to close.

4. Starting at the top of the cone, insert an Eastern white pinecone to create the tip (Figure C). Continue to insert the cones evenly into the chicken wire spaces. Use thinner, shorter, smaller cones at the top, working the larger cones toward the bottom. Be careful not to pack the cones too tightly or they won't be able to open. If some of the cones become loose as you continue, simply reinforce them by placing soft, tiny cones around them. In cases where some cones will not remain stationary, wire the cones directly to the wire frame.

5. As the cones dry, they will open, reinforcing and filling in the empty spaces. Glue in additional nuts or pods if desired.

6. Spray the entire tree with two coats of spray gloss varnish.

7. When completely dry, glue wheat and small pieces of gyp evenly over the tree. Add a butterfly bow made from the brown velvet ribbon at the base of the tree.

Note: This tree can also be adapted as a wall or door decoration. Make only half the tree, leaving the back flat to remain flush against the wall. Use half a basket for the base. Follow the same procedure as above to insert pinecones.

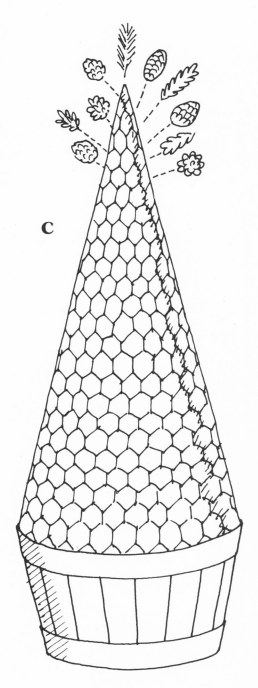

DOUBLE PINECONE WREATH

MATERIALS

Sugar-pine cones
2 metal wreath frames, 18″ and
    16″ diameter
Pinecone flowerettes
Assorted varieties, shapes, and sizes
    of pinecones
Medium wire

Household bleach
Nuts
Linoleum adhesive
Spray gloss varnish
Dried gypsophila (baby's breath)
Floral glue
Heavy Wire

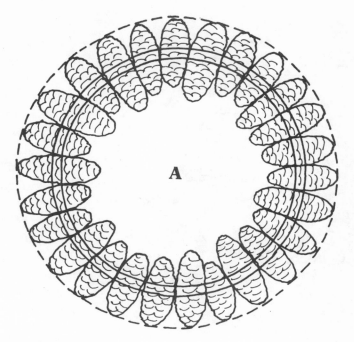

A

1. Soak the sugar cones in water until they close. Place cones of approximately the same size and length into the side of the 18″ frame. Make sure that the outside edge of the cones, not the inside rim, is circular and even (Figure A). Do not worry if the inside is uneven; it will be covered with the 16″ wreath later. Allow the cones to dry and open. Follow the same procedure with the smaller wreath, allowing the cones to dry only partially.

2. Wire all the other pinecones individually with a 13″ length of wire. To create interesting composition and texture for your wreath, use the top, bottom, and sides of the cones. Also incorporate flowerettes. Additional color contrast can be achieved by bleaching some of the cones.

3. After you wire all the cones, place three different kinds of cones together in a cluster. Twist the three wires tightly together.

103

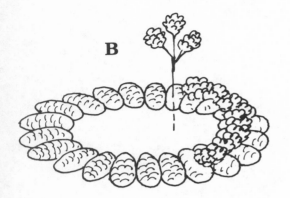

B

4. Place the clusters closely on the top of the 16″ wreath, inserting the wires through the semi-opened sugar cones (Figure B). Attach the wires to the back of the metal frame. You can use a giant needle, available in many craft stores, to make this process easier.

5. When the top part of your wreath is full, you can add nuts and additional cones where needed. Dip one end of each nut or cone into linoleum adhesive, set them in place, and allow to dry.

6. When the smaller wreath is completely finished, place it evenly on top of the 18″ wreath. Use heavy wire to loop between both metal frames, holding them together securely (Figure C).

7. Add single cones between the first and second wreath, using linoleum adhesive. These cones fill in the spaces between the two wreaths, so that the two frames appear to be one.

8. Provide the finish to your wreath by spraying it with two or three coats of spray gloss varnish.

9. When your wreath is completely dry, glue small pieces of dry gyp (baby's breath) evenly over the cones.

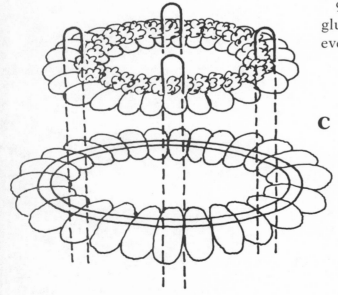

C

FOUR

Holiday Collection

GRANDFATHER CLOCK

See also color plate 17

MATERIALS

32"-square sheet corrugated cardboard
Newspaper or thin cardboard
Hacksaw or serrated knife
Stapler
Floral glue
7 yards 2¾"-wide woven plaid ribbon (or any plaid fabric)
Razor blade
6 yards 1½"-wide cotton lace
12"-square 1"-thick Styrofoam
1"-diameter empty fabric roll
½ yard red corduroy
Masking tape
White paint

Cutting pliers
Thin metal chain (available hardware or lumber stores)
Wire or hairpins
Clear, thin sheet of plastic (optional)
1 florist funeral clock (available from florist or cemetery dump). Or you can make your own from posterboard and decal numbers.
Posterboard.
Black paint.
1 ball fringe
1 ruler

A

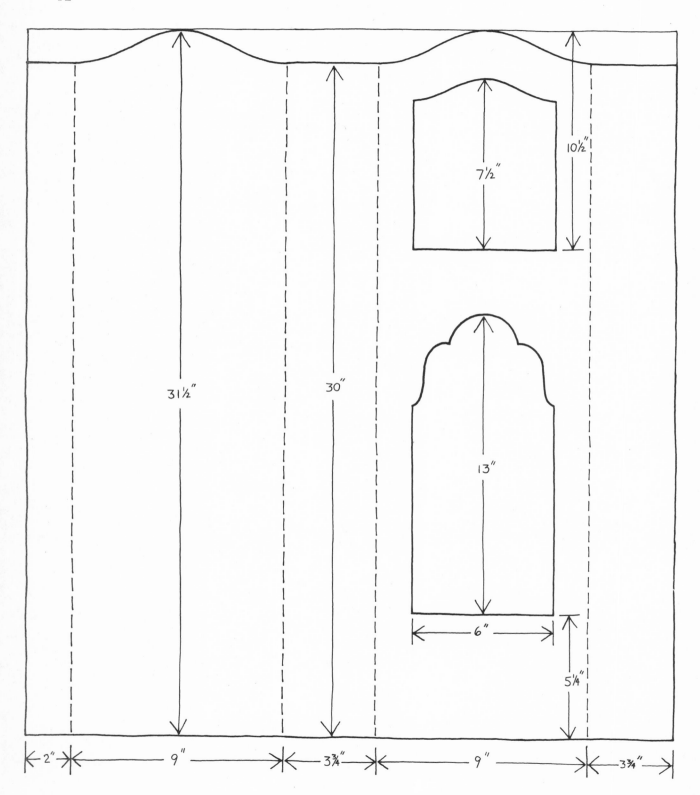

Clock Body

1. Reproduce the pattern shown according to the corrugated cardboard (Figure A).

2. Cut windows and top of the clock carefully with a hacksaw or serrated knife. Next, turn the cardboard over and place a straight edge along the dotted lines. With a pen point, slightly indent the cardboard along the edge. Fold the creases back, placing the excess 2″ segment inside (Figure B). After you have formed the clock case staple the excess securely in place.

3. Glue the ribbon, starting with the sides closest to the back. Match the plaids as much as possible. Place the second row of ribbon, lapping the excess over to the front of the clock (it should end at the 1½″ margin). If you use fabric instead of ribbon, cut one piece large enough to cover the front and the sides. Cut out the insides around the windows, leaving a 1″ seam. Glue this excess to the inside of the windows. Fill in the empty spaces on the front of the clock with the remaining ribbon. Match plaids. Trim the edges around the window with a razor blade. Glue the lace trim around the clock windows. Square the corners neatly.

4. Cut a 11½″ x 5″ piece out of the Styrofoam for the base. Cover the sides and 1″ along the top edge with ribbon (Figure C).

B

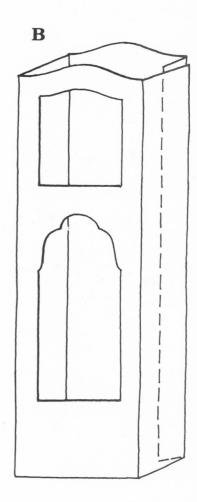

C

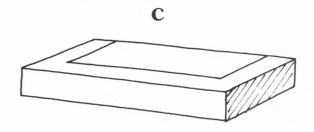

D

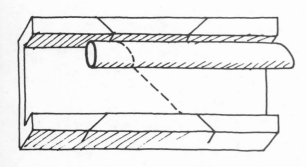

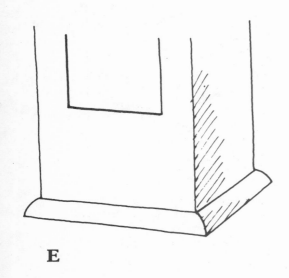

E

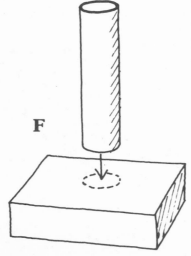

F

5. Cut three lengths from the fabric roll: one piece at 10½", two pieces at 4½". Cut each roll vertically in half with a hacksaw. Place the corners in a miter box and miter the front corners only (Figure D).

6. Glue the molding to the front along the bottom of the clock (Figure E). If the corners are not perfect, cover them with masking tape, cutting off the excess. Cover the entire molding with corduroy fabric. Trim the edges with a razor blade. Place lace trim on the top of the molding.

7. Glue corduroy to the inside of the lower clock window only. Starting 2" above the window, continue the fabric to the bottom of the clock, covering both the back and the sides.

Clock Movement

1. For the chimes, cut three lengths from the fabric roll, each 4" long. For the top of the chimes, force the open end of the roll into a 1"-thick piece of Styrofoam (Figure F). Remove the Styrofoam segment. Put glue around the Styrofoam and re-insert it in place. Cover the entire chime with ribbon. Place lace trim around the top and the bottom of the chime. Spray the chain with white paint. Use cutting pliers to cut two lengths at 5" and one each at 3", 15", and 12". Loop wires or hairpins into the last loop of the three shortest chains. Insert and glue into the top of the chimes.

2. For the pendulum, cut a piece 10″ x ½″ from corrugated cardboard (Figure G). Paint white. When dry, cover with two strands of thin lace, one on each side. Cut a circle 2½″ in diameter from cardboard. Cover with ribbon and place lace trim around the edge. Glue the circle to the end of the 10″ strip.

Assembly

1. To assemble the entire "movement section," cut a 9″ x 1½″ piece from the remaining Styrofoam. Using the same hairpin or wire procedure through all the chains, as in Step 8, place the two 5″ chains, 3″ inward from the ends of the Styrofoam (Figure H). Glue the 3″ chain in the center and the two remaining chains on either side of it. Glue the pendulum on the back of the Styrofoam. Before you insert the entire movement section, cut two sheets of plastic, 15″ x 8″ and 8″ x 9″, and glue them on the inside of the windows. This step can be eliminated, if desired.

2. To insert the movement section, place the glue inside 1″ from the bottom of the top window. Place the 9″ Styrofoam section over the glue. Insert hairpins from the front of the clock into the Styrofoam to hold in place until dry.

3. For the inside top window, cut an 8½″ x 10″ piece of corrugated cardboard. Cover with red corduroy, leaving ½″ excess at the bottom.

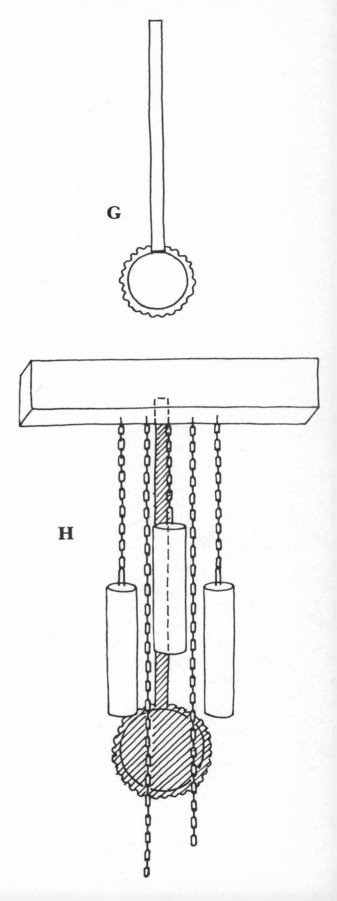

G

H

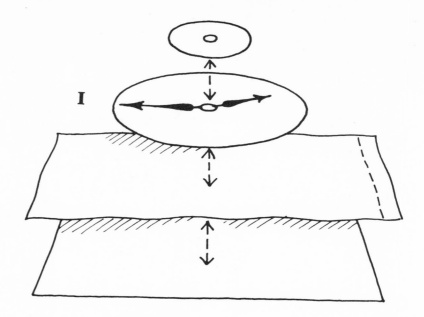

I

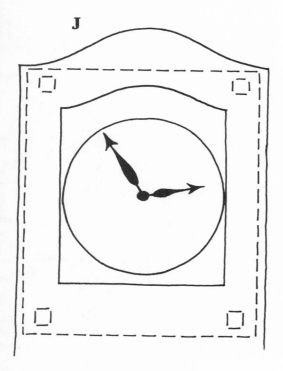

J

4. For the clock face, repaint the florist funeral clock white; repaint the numbers and the hands with black paint or thick felt-tip pen.

Note: You can also make your own clock face from a 6″ posterboard circle. Add stick-on numbers. Cut out hands and paint them black. Cut a 2½″ circle from corrugated cardboard. Cover with ribbon. Glue the disk to the center of the clock face (Figure I). Glue thin lace around the edge of the 2½″ circle. Glue the completed clock face to the 10″ x 8½″ piece of cardboard, 1¾″ from the bottom. Cover the edge of the 6″ circle with lace trim.

Add 1 ball fringe in the center of the hands.

5. Next, place a small amount of glue on the top of the large Styrofoam piece inside. Slowly place the completed clock face onto the Styrofoam. The ½″ excess corduroy should rest evenly along the top. Cut a 1″ Styrofoam square. Cut lengthwise in half, and glue each piece into the upper corners of the 10″ panel (Figure J). Glue the panel to the inside front of the clock.

Color Plate 17   Clocks: Left, Grandfather Clock, page 107; top center, Alarm Clock, page 127; bottom center, Schoolhouse Clock, page 122; right, Cuckoo Clock, page 131

Color Plate 19   Ribbons and Fringe Centerpiece, page 139

Color Plate 18   Popcorn and Cranberry: Left to right, Bouquet, page 188; Nosegay, 190; Tree Basket, page 190

Color Plate 20
Kissing Ball, page 142

Color Plate 21
Victorian Blue Ornament,
page 180

Color Plate 22   Country Plaid Wreath, page 136

Color Plate 23   Pinecone Tree, page 99

Color Plate 24   Peppermint and Cherries Jubilee, page 144

Color Plate 25   Old-Fashioned Goodies, page 161

6. For the molding on the top of the clock, make three patterns from corrugated cardboard (Figure K). Cut out patterns and glue the three evenly together. Glue along the front of the top arc.

7. Cut two 4¼" x 1" pieces of Styrofoam. Along one 4" edge, place a ruler ¼" inward from the edge and mark with a pen firmly along the Styrofoam edge (about ¼" deep) (Figure L). Glue the two pieces on either side at the top of the clock, placing evenly with the three front moldings. Glue red corduroy to the entire molding, folding the excess underneath.

8. Cut an 11½" x 4½" piece from the posterboard. Glue it to the top of the clock. Cover with corduroy, with white upholstery gimp over the seams. Glue the base onto the bottom of the clock.

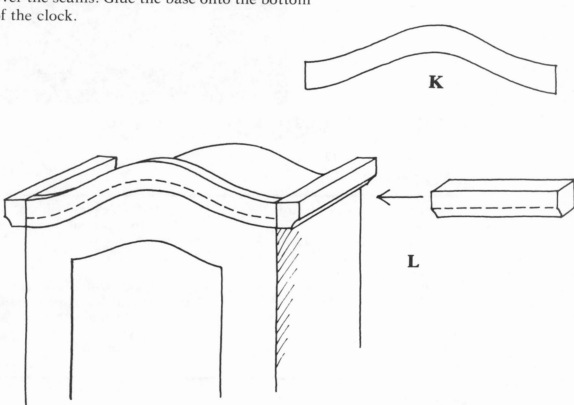

K

L

SCHOOLHOUSE CLOCK

See also color plate 17

MATERIALS

Newspaper or thin cardboard	5 yards 1½"-wide plaid ribbon
Scissors	6" x 12" strip white cardboard
2 pieces 1"-thick Styrofoam, 10" square and 9" square	Black paint
	White paint
Hacksaw	Razor blade
Yardstick	1 yard ¼" wide cotton lace trim
16" x 11" corrugated cardboard	Florist funeral clock or poster-board (see "Grandfather Clock")
Serrated knife	
Masking tape	3 yards ½"-wide cotton lace trim
Floral glue	Chenille stem or wire
¼ yard red corduroy	Stapler

Face

1. To make the pattern for the outer octagon, use a compass to make a 10″ circle on a piece of newspaper (Figure A-1). Divide the circle into four even pie pieces. When complete, divide the 4 pieces into 8 pieces. Connect the points as shown with a straight line. Cut out the octagon pattern and place it on the 10″ Styrofoam square. Cut the pattern carefully with a hacksaw blade.

Note: You must hold the blade straight when cutting or the sides will angle inward. It's not hard. Just take your time.

2. Fold the pattern again. To make the 9″ pattern, simply cut off ½″ along the two open sides of the pattern. Open the pattern and trace onto the 9″ square Styrofoam. Cut carefully with hacksaw.

3. On 9″ octagon only (using a yardstick and pencil or fine felt-tip pen) make a smaller octagon on the top of the Styrofoam by measuring ¾″ inward from the edges (Figure A-2). When you have completed the top, follow the same procedure on the sides of the 9″ square; measure 3′ 4″ upward from the sides of the octagon.

4. Next, angle the hacksaw blade on the two lines. Carefully bevel the Styrofoam edge around the entire octagon (Figure A-2). Cut very slowly and evenly, cutting as close as possible to the lines. If your bevel is uneven, use a Styrofoam scrap to "sandpaper" the bevel until it is uniform. Be sure that all your bevels are uniform (Figure A-3).

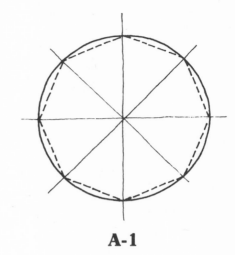

A-1

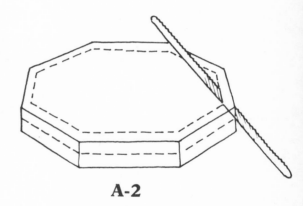

A-2

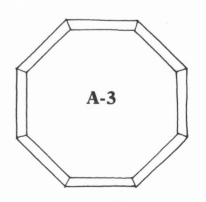

A-3

B

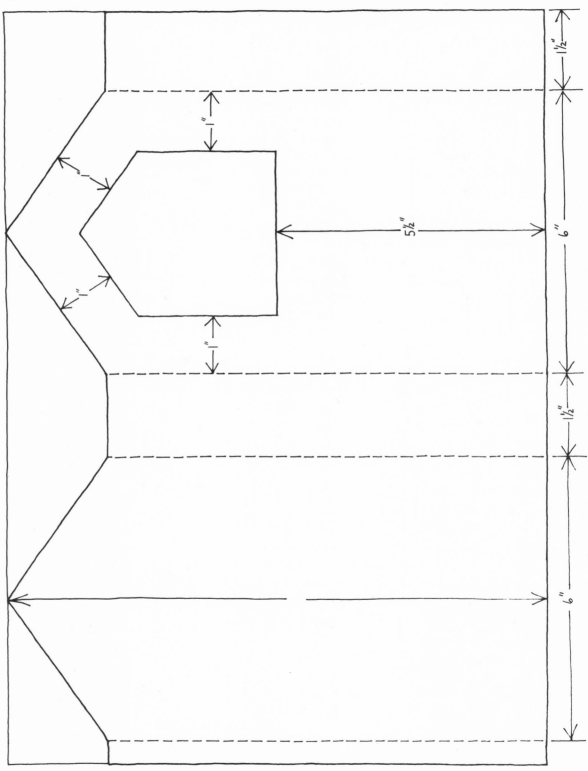

Body

1. Duplicate the pattern for the lower part of the clock on the corrugated cardboard. Cut on dark, heavy lines only with a serrated knife (Figure B).

When you have completed it, turn cardboard over. Place the yardstick edge along the dotted lines. With a pen point, slightly indent the cardboard along the dotted lines. (This provides an even seam for the bending.) Bend each side along the seam, forming the bottom of the clock (Figure C). Use masking tape to secure the two ends together.

2. Cut a 1¾" strip of cardboard and tape it to cover the open end at the bottom (Figure C). Cut ½" strips of cardboard and glue them along the rim of the pendulum view box.

Assembly

1. Glue the red corduroy on the top of the 9" octagon, leaving a ¼" excess along the edge to fold onto the bevel. This excess will be covered by the ribbon. Make a slit in each corner of the corduroy and glue the fabric down evenly.

2. Glue the plaid ribbon along the 1" edge of the 10" octagon to cover it. Do not cut off the excess ribbon that remains upright. Cut a slit in the ribbon at each corner, stopping at the top of the Styrofoam edge.

3. Place glue on the corner below the slip. Pinch the two slit ends together (Figure D). Lay the seam firmly on the Styrofoam. Follow the same procedure at each corner, gluing in between as you go along. Press firmly on both sides of the seam, using your fingernail, to eliminate any spaces when the excess is cut off.

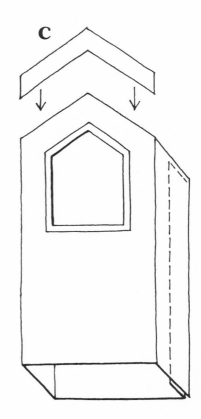

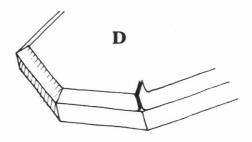

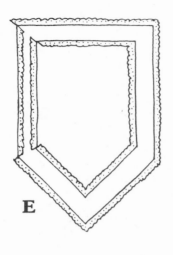

E

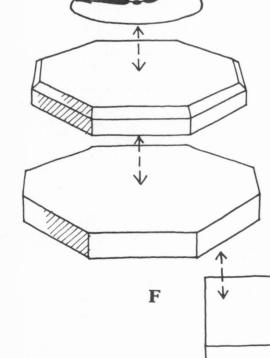

F

4. Allow to dry. With a razor blade, cut off the excess neatly at the corners so that the seam is flush with the rest of the ribbon. Follow the same procedure for the 9″ octagon.

5. Cover the cardboard section with ribbon. Start from the sides and work your way toward the front. Match the plaid as much as possible. For the corners at the bottom of the clock, follow the same procedure as above.

6. Cover the ½″ cardboard window border with ribbon. Glue the ¼″ lace trim to the outside and inside of the border (Figure E). Cut and glue a small piece of corduroy to fit inside the back of the clock window. Cut a 1½″-diameter circle from cardboard. Cover it with ribbon. Glue the ¼″ lace trim around the edge of the circle.

7. Glue the circle to the end of a 6″ x ½″ strip of white cardboard. Glue the strip inside the view box so that the pendulum can be seen. You can attach the strip to a small piece of Styrofoam, if you wish to elevate it.

8. To make the clock face, see "Grandfather Clock," page 111. Glue the completed face on the center of the 9″ octagon (Figure F). Glue the 9″ octagon to the center of the 10″ octagon. Next, glue the ½″ lace trim facing outward, along the back of the 10″ octagon. Last, glue the lace along the back of the cardboard segment.

9. To hang, loop a wire or chenille stem to the cardboard back. Staple securely in place.

ALARM CLOCK

See also color plate 17

MATERIALS

2"-thick Styrofoam, enough to cut 2 circles 9" in diameter
Hacksaw
Floral glue
4 yards 2¾"-wide plaid ribbon
6"-diameter Styrofoam ball
Razor blade
3 yards ¼"-wide cotton lace trim
¼ yard red corduroy
1½ yards ½"-wide double-edge cotton lace trim

3 2"-diameter red flocked Christmas balls (or cover Styrofoam balls with strips of corduroy)
½"-thick ceiling foam or Styrofoam, 7" square
Florist funeral clock or posterboard (see Grandfather Clock, page 112)
1½ yards ½"-wide cotton lace
White pencil or dowel
Round toothpicks

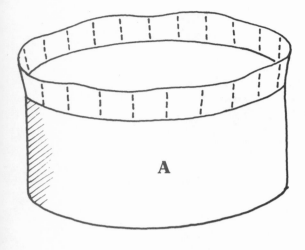

A

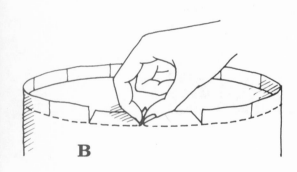

B

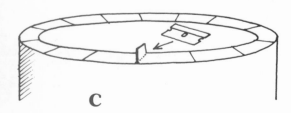

C

1. Cut two 9″ circles from the Styrofoam. Cut evenly with a hacksaw. Keep the blade straight when cutting or the sides of the circle will angle inward and become uneven.

2. Glue the two circles together. If the sides are uneven, bevel with a small piece of Styrofoam as you would with sandpaper until the edges are uniform.

3. Glue the ribbon to the circles, starting at the bottom of the sides. After you glue the first row, apply the second row, matching plaids as much as possible. Do not cut off the ribbon that remains upright. Cut small slits every 2″ along the top of the ribbon (Figure A). The slit should end at the top of the circle.

4. Place some glue on the Styrofoam below each slit. Pinch the two slit ends together so they make a seam and lay the seam firmly on the Styrofoam (Figure B). Press firmly with your fingernails on both sides of the slit to eliminate any spaces when the excess is cut off. Follow the same procedure for each slit, gluing in between the slits as you go along.

5. With a razor blade, cut off the excess neatly at each slit so that the seam is flush with the rest of the ribbon (Figure C). If any spaces remain, fill them in with shredded ribbon.

6. For the top of the alarm clock, cut the 6″ Styrofoam ball in half (one half is all you need). Cut the remaining plaid ribbon lengthwise in half. Cut the ribbon into 3″ lengths. Glue the first strip, starting from the base of the ball, working the ribbon upward. Try to match plaids as much as possible.

7. As you apply the second strip and each subsequent strip, the upper part of the ribbon should overlap the previous strip (Figure D). Pinch the seams together as you did on the front of the clock. Place glue under each seam. Press firmly on each side of the seam with your fingernail. When the glue is dry, use a razor blade to cut off the excess neatly. Follow the same procedure around the entire ball.

8. Cover the remaining exposed part of the ball, using "pie pieces" (Figure E). When the entire dome is covered, cover the seams vertically with two pieces of ¼"-wide lace back to back, or one piece of ½"-wide double-edge lace (Figure F). Start at the top of the ball, working down to the bottom.

9. Cover the bottom of the ball with red corduroy. Glue the lace trim around its base. Insert a round toothpick into one red flocked ball. Place that ball on the top of the Styrofoam ball. Glue securely in place.

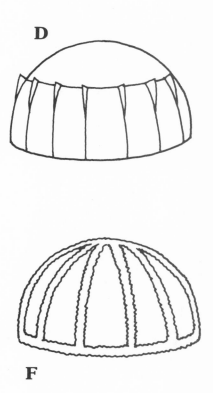

D

F

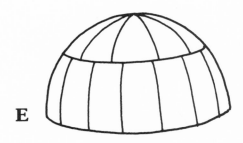

E

10. For clock face see "Grandfather Clock," page 111. Cut a 6"-diameter circle from the ceiling foam or Styrofoam. Glue the completed clock face on the top of the Styrofoam circle (Figure G). Cut a 7½"-diameter circle from posterboard. Cover this circle with corduroy. Glue the ½"-wide lace trim around the edge. Glue the 6" foam circle to the 7½" circle. Glue the entire face on the front of the clock.

Assembly

1. Insert a short white pencil or dowel into the top of the clock, then underneath the center of the Styrofoam ball. Glue the dowel in place.

2. For the legs, place two flocked balls on the bottom of the clock by securing them with round toothpicks and glue.

3. Add a short dowel to the back of the clock to serve as a rest so that the clock remains upright.

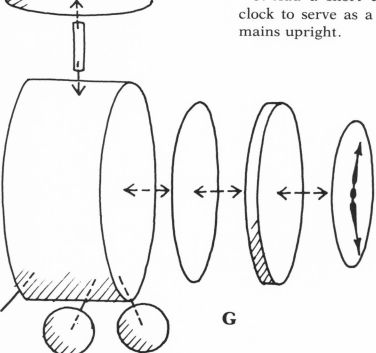

G

CUCKOO CLOCK

See also color plate 17

MATERIALS:

26″ x 13½″ corrugated cardboard
Serrated knife
Yardstick
Stapler
Masking tape
Floral glue
5 yards 2¾″-wide woven plaid ribbon
Razor blade
½″ ceiling foam or Styrofoam, 7″ square
70″ metal chain (available in hardware or lumber stores)
Wire
¼ yard medium-size green ball fringe
2 long super pinecones
½″-wide cotton lace trim
1 yard white satin roping
2″ white bird (available in dime stores or Christmas supply houses)
Florist funeral clock or posterboard (see "Grandfather Clock", page 112)
White spray paint

A

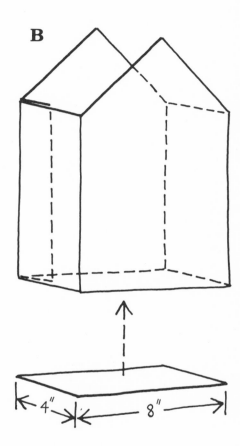

1. Reproduce the pattern shown according to the dimensions given, using corrugated cardboard (Figure A). With a serrated knife, cut on the heavy black lines of the pattern only. When complete, turn the cardboard over and place the yardstick edge along the dotted lines. With a pen point, slightly indent the cardboard along the dotted lines.

2. Fold the crease back, forming the cardboard into the clock shape (Figure B). Place the excess 2″ segment inside the clock and staple together securely. Cut a 4″ x 8″ piece of cardboard. Place it at the open end of the clock at the bottom. Secure the cardboard to the clock with masking tape around the edges.

3. Glue the ribbon vertically to the clock, starting in the center on the front and working your way to the sides. Cover the doors as well. Try to match the plaids as much as possible. Start on the front at the peak and work across to the sides, ending with a small excess in the back. (Do not glue the bottom or the back in place yet.) When you are gluing the ribbon on the sides only, extend the ribbon ½″ to the bottom of the clock and glue in place. After you glue the ribbon on both sides, glue the ribbon to the bottom.

4. When the entire clock is covered with ribbon, use a razor blade to cut the ribbon along the edges of the door. Glue ribbon to the inside of the door.

5. Follow directions for the "Grandfather Clock," p. 111, for the clock face. Cut a 6″ circle from the ceiling foam or Styrofoam. Glue the clock face on the circle. Glue the completed face on the front of the clock.

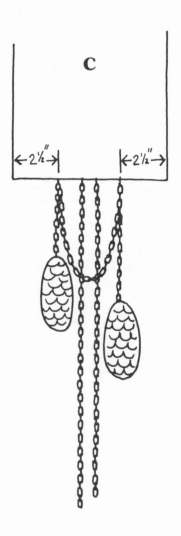

C

←2½"→   ←2½"→

6. Cut the chain in three lengths: 24", 22", and 21". Paint the two pinecones and three chains with white paint. Wrap a wire around the last layer of petals on the two pinecones. Twist the wire to the base of the cone. Place a small piece of wire through the last loop of the longest chain. Attach the wire from the loop to the wire of the pinecone.

7. Measure 4" of chain from the pinecone (Figure C). At this point, loop a 5" length of wire through the chain. Insert the wire into the bottom of the clock, about 2½" inward from the left side. Secure the wire to the inside cardboard with masking tape.

8. Measure 13" of chain from that point, form a loop with the chain (see photo), and insert a wire through the chain. Place the wire through the bottom of the clock, 2½" inward from the right side. After you tape the wire in place, attach the remaining pinecone to the end of the chain. Glue a small bow with a ball fringe in the center on the top of the pinecones. Add the two remaining chains, inserting them as above with wire. Glue a ball fringe to the end of each chain.

9. For the top of the clock, cut a 15" x 4½" piece of corrugated cardboard. Cover one side entirely with ribbon, leaving a 3" overlap in the back on both ends (Figure D). Bend the cardboard evenly in half. Glue it on the top of the clock. Glue the lace trim along the front edge of the cardboard. Glue the satin roping slightly above the lace trim.

10. Cut a 2″ x 2″ arc from a scrap of corrugated cardboard for the bird to rest upon at the door opening (Figure E). Cover it with corduroy. Bend ½″ of the cardboard downward at the straight end. Glue the entire arc to the inside bottom of the doors. Next, glue the lace trim on the doors and arc. Last, glue the bird on the arc. Place the lace trim around the front seams of the clock.

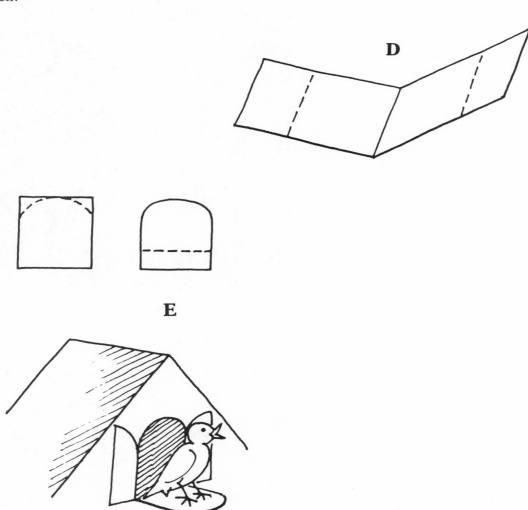

D

E

COUNTRY PLAID WREATH

See also color plate 22

MATERIALS

15″-diameter Styrofoam wreath
Real or artificial pine and greens
7½ yards 1½″-wide plaid woven ribbon
5 2¾″ x 4¼″ rectangles of 1″-thick Styrofoam (Vary sizes slightly so they look like packages)
Floral glue
4 yards unruffled white eyelet trim
1½ yards ⅜″-wide red velvet ribbon
Straight pins (optional)

8 white or green chenille stems
3″ and 4″ florist picks
12 2″-diameter Styrofoam balls
4 yards ½″-wide lace trim or edging
20 to 25 1″-diameter Styrofoam balls
Scraps of red corduroy (¼ yard)
2 yards tiny white ball fringe
Medium wire
White medical tape
Stapler
Green floral tape

1. Using the procedure for making a Styrofoam wreath (p. 24), insert the real or artificial pine and greens shown there.

2. To cover the packages, cut 2 feet of the 1½" plaid ribbon cut lengthwise in half. Glue this ribbon along the sides of the five packages. Glue on any combination of eyelet, plaid, and velvet ribbon for the top of the packages. You could also use straight pins in place of the glue. Cut three chenille stems in half. Form a loop with each half and insert the ends, 2½" apart, into the back of the Styrofoam. Twist the loop and place it on a 4" florist pick.

3. To cover the 2" Styrofoam balls, cut strips of plaid ribbon ½" wide. Cut three lengths to cover one half of the ball (only one half will be visible). Glue the first ribbon down the center of the ball (Figure A). Apply the two remaining ribbons on either side of center, leaving less than ½" space between each strip. Glue the lace trim over the two spaces between the plaid strips (Figure B). Wrap lace along one half the edge of the ball. Cut 3" pieces from the five remaining chenille stems. Glue each piece to the back of each ball. Place the stems on a 3" or 4" florist pick.

4. To cover the 1" Styrofoam balls, cut 4" squares from the red corduroy. Place each ball in the center of each square and twist the fabric tightly around the ball. Wrap a wire around the twist. Cover the exposed wire with floral tape.

5. To make the plaid flowers, see "Ribbons and Fringe," p. 140. Make 25 plaid flowers.

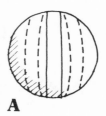

A

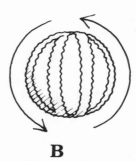

B

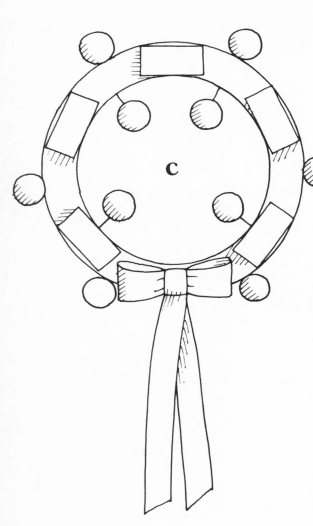

C

6. To assemble the entire wreath, place the packages and the large Styrofoam balls on 3″ or 4″ picks and insert them into the wreath (Figure C). Place the small balls and the plaid flowers on 3″ or 4″ picks and insert them evenly throughout the wreath in between the packages and balls. Cut the remaining ball fringe from the string and glue the individual balls evenly over the wreath.

7. To make the bow, cut five lengths from the plaid ribbon; 15″, 20″, two at 8″, and one at 4″. Glue the eyelet along both edges of the ribbon strips. Extend the eyelet approximately ¾″ from the edge of the ribbon as shown in color plate 12. Place a wire lengthwise down the center of the adhesive side of the medical tape. Place the wired tape on the back of the two 8″ pieces and the one 4″ piece of ribbon. Bring the ends of each 8″ segment together, forming a loop (Figure D). Place each loop on a 3″ or 4″ pick. Insert the two loops into the wreath, creating a bow. Put each end of the 4″ segment on a 3″ pick. Place the ribbon in the middle of the bow, inserting the picks into the Styrofoam, above and below the bow. Staple the two streamers together and glue them underneath the bow. Glue ball fringe along the bottom of the streamers, if you wish.

RIBBONS AND FRINGE

See also color plate 19

MATERIALS

1-gallon paint can, or a round box, or a cookie tin, 4″ high, and 8″ diameter. (Any type of container can be used for your arrangement. It's hard to find a less costly container than an empty paint can.)

Metal cutting shears

Masking tape

5 to 6 yards 1½″-wide plaid ribbon

1½ yards ⅜″-wide red velvet ribbon

Floral glue

1½ yards 1½″-wide double-edge white cotton eyelet

3 to 8 yards white ball fringe

Medium wire

3 to 4 dozen artificial boxwood or tea-leaf greens

Real or artificial pine

Assorted-size florist picks

Round toothpicks

Green floral tape

White medical tape

3 to 3½″-diameter Styrofoam ball

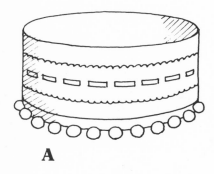

A

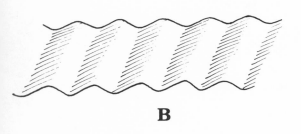

B

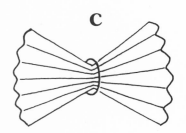

C

1. Measure 4″ up from the bottom of the container you are using if it is taller than 4″. Measure around it. Use metal cutting shears to cut evenly around the container. When you are finished, cover the cut edges of container with masking tape to avoid any injury from the sharp edges.

2. Glue a strip of plaid ribbon around the top and bottom of the can (Figure A). Weave the ⅜″ velvet ribbon through the eyelet. Then, in the remaining center space glue the eyelet between the two strips of ribbon. Glue the ball fringe around the base of the can.

3. To create the flowers, cut 3″ strips from the remaining plaid ribbon. When you have pleated the entire piece of ribbon (Figure B), loop an 8″ length of wire around the center of the pleats (Figure C). Twist the ends of the wire securely in back. Glue a white ball fringe in the center of each flower.

Assembly

1. Using three or four dozen 3″ boxwood or tea-leaf greens, insert the stems directly into the Styrofoam ball (Figure D). Cover two-thirds of the ball evenly with the greens. If you want your sphere shape to look airy and less stylized, add small pieces of real or artificial hemlock to soften the design.

2. Place the wired flowers on round toothpicks (or 3″ florist picks), securing the wires with floral tape. Insert the flowers, spacing them evenly into the ball (Figure E). Maintain the sphere design.

3. For the single-ball fringe, loop a medium wire through the metal clasp in the center of the ball fringe. Twist the wires in back. Place

the wired ball fringe on round toothpicks and insert into the Styrofoam. Or glue the ball fringe directly on the greens.

Bow

1. Weave the remaining velvet ribbon through the remaining eyelet.

2. Since most cotton eyelet is too limp to hold a firm bow, you can use white medical tape and wire for body. Tape the wire all the way down the middle of the adhesive side of the tape.

3. Place the wired tape on the back of the eyelet. Make a cross bow, using the remaining ribbon as a streamer. Wrap wire through the center of the bow and the streamer. Twist securely in back.

4. Place the wired bow on top of the bouquet (Figure F). Weave the streamers through the greens.

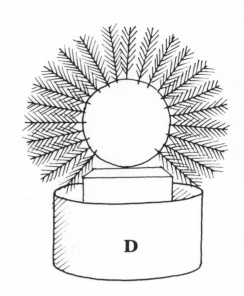

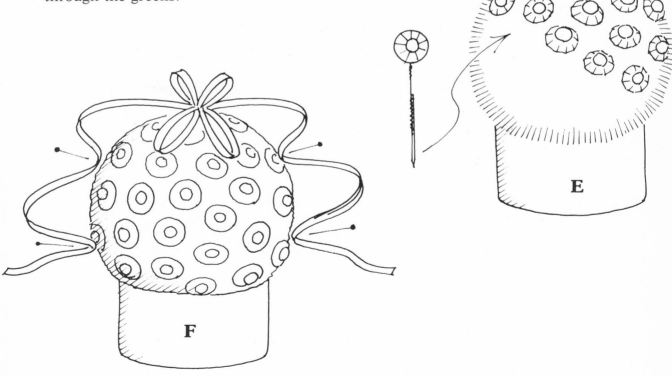

KISSING BALL

See also color plate 20

MATERIALS

3 yards red string pom-poms
½ yard white string pom-poms
6"-diameter Styrofoam ball
Glue
5 yards 2 shades of green (olive and moss) string pom-poms (pom-poms are available in drapery trimming departments)

2 yards ⅝"-wide ribbon, stripe, plaid, or polka dot
2 yards 1½"-wide double-edge eyelet
White medical tape
Wire
3" florist picks
Scissors

142

1. Glue eighteen flower patterns to the Styrofoam ball. Make these by arranging five red pom-poms in a circle, with one white pom-pom in the center. Space the eighteen patterns evenly over the ball (Figure A).

2. Fill in the remaining spaces with the green pom-poms. Space the two shades of green evenly over the ball, gluing the pom-poms in place as you go along.

3. To make the bow, glue the ribbon down the center of the double-edge eyelet.

4. Make the bow as in "Ribbons and Fringe," p. 141, using white medical tape and wire for body.

5. Place the wired tape on the back of the eyelet. Cut five 6″ lengths of wired eyelet. Form a loop with each strip and place each loop on a 3″ pick.

6. Create your own bow by inserting the five loops, in a circular manner, at the top of the Styrofoam ball. Cut three 3″ streamers. Place on picks and insert through the bow. Cut a 20″ length of eyelet ribbon without wire. Form a loop, place on a 3″ pick, and insert into the center of the bow.

7. For ribbon below the Kissing Ball, make one loop with two streamers. Place on a 3″ pick and insert into the bottom of the ball. Glue a pom-pom on the bottom edge of each streamer.

Note: You can make a variation of this project to use as a tree ornament by using a smaller Styrofoam ball and tiny ball fringe.

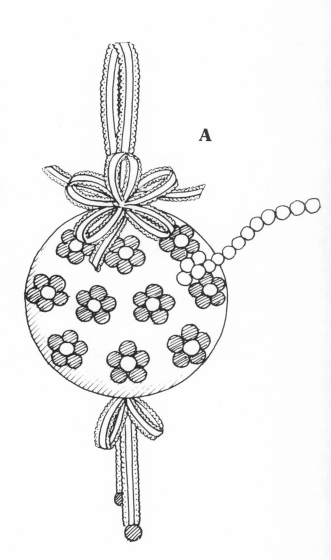

A

FABULOUS FAKES: PEPPERMINT AND CHERRIES JUBILEE

See also color plate 24

MATERIALS

Creative clay (see recipe)
15 moss-green chenille stems
Floral glue
3 yards ⅝"-wide striped grosgrain ribbon
2 rattan mats 12" and 16" in diameter
White ceiling paint
White spray paint
4" square 2" Styrofoam
6" scrap red corduroy or fabric
Medium wire
Thin wire
14"-diameter Styrofoam wreath
Heavy wire, greening pins, or hairpins
1½ yards 1½"-wide red cotton polka dot ribbon
6" circle 1" green Styrofoam

3" and 4" florist picks
Green floral tape
Round toothpicks
6 polka dot cloth flowers (or make your own from additional ribbon or fabric)
3½ yards 1½"-wide striped grosgrain ribbon
1¼"-diameter plastic prescription pill bottle (or the plastic case that holds a roll of film)
½"-diameter felt-tip pen or marker cap
2 36" wooden dowels, ½" diameter (available in any lumber store), or old cut-up pencils
34 1"-diameter Styrofoam balls
Red cellophane
Artificial or real pine and greens

Creative Clay Recipe

In a saucepan, stir thoroughly 1 cup of cornstarch and 2 cups of baking soda (the contents of a 1-pound package). Mix in 1¼ cups of cold water. Heat, stirring constantly, until mixture reaches a slightly moist, mashed-potato consistency. Turn out on a plate and cover with a damp cloth. When cool enough to handle, knead like dough. Add a few drops of hand cream, mixing it thoroughly into the mixture, to make the mixture a little smoother and to prevent cracking.

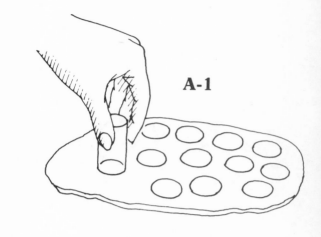

A-1

Lifesavers: After kneading the dough, place it on top of a sheet of wax paper. Roll the dough approximately ½" thick, using a rolling pin. The top of the dough must be smooth and even. To create the outer circle of the Lifesavers, simply insert the open end of the pill bottle into the dough (Figure A-1). For the inner circle, press a felt marker cap or felt-tip pen cap into the center of the larger circle (Figure A-2). Lift the clay gently. All that should remain on the wax paper are the Lifesavers (Figure A-3). Make 36 Lifesavers. When they are dry, cut 12 chenille stems into 4" segments. Glue each stem across the back of each Lifesaver. The moss-colored chenille stem showing through the center of the Lifesaver will not be visible when inserted among the greens.

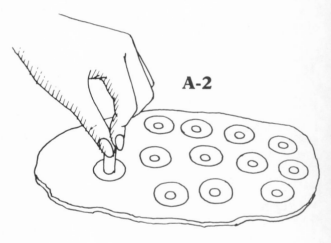

A-2

Peppermint Sticks: See "Old-Fashioned Goodies," p. 164.

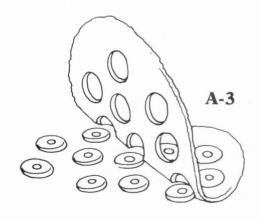

A-3

Ribbon Candy: Cut twelve 9″ lengths from the ⅝″ grosgrain ribbon. Place a small amount of glue on the end of a length of ribbon (Figure B-1). Weave the ribbon, making a single loop (Figure B-2). Continue to loop the ribbon back and forth, placing a small amount of glue on the alternate loops (Figure B-3). Make 12. When they are complete, glue a 4″ chenille stem lengthwise across the back of each candy.

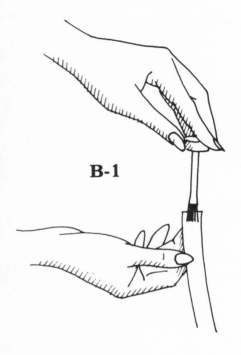

B-1

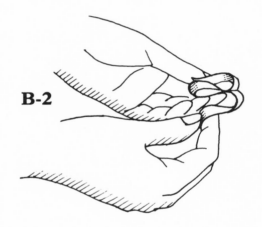

B-2

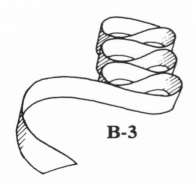

B-3

Cherry Balls: Cut a 3½" x 3½" square of red corduroy. Place a 1" Styrofoam ball in the center of the square (Figure C-1). Pull the four corners together, twisting the cellophane tightly in back (Figure C-2). Place the twist in the center of a 6" length of medium wire. Wrap the wire around the twist (Figure C-3). Cover the complete twist with florist tape to hold securely (Figure C-4). Follow the same procedure for all the balls. Make 34.

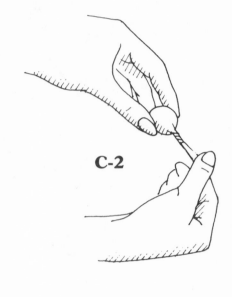

C-2

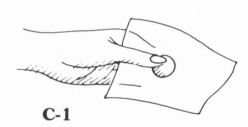

C-1

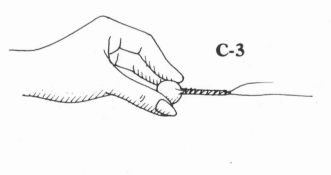

C-3

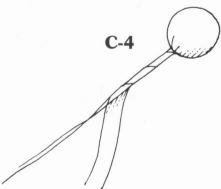

C-4

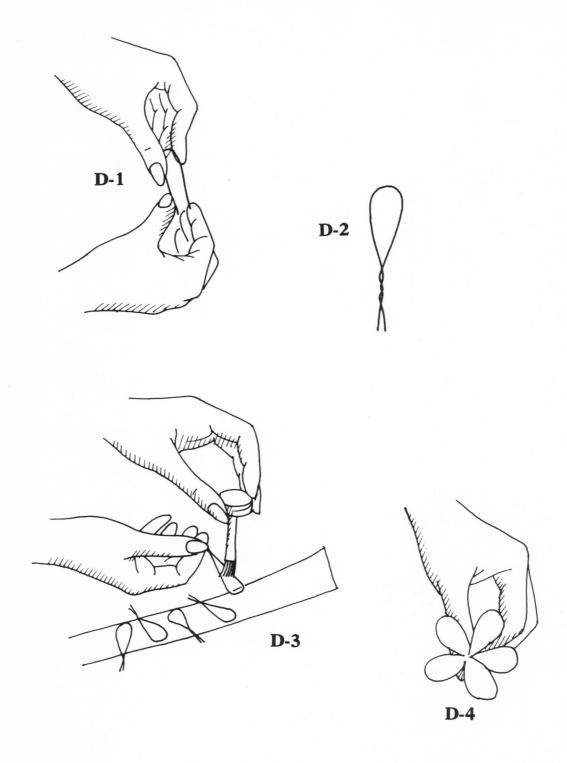

D-1

D-2

D-3

D-4

Polka Dot Flowers: If you make your own flowers, you need an additional yard of cotton polka dot ribbon or very stiffly starched fabric; medium wire; tiny black or white ball fringe. Cut thirty 4½″ pieces of medium wire. Bend the two ends of the wire together, forming a petal (Figures D-1 and D-2). Place glue on the entire wire petal and place it on the reverse side of the ribbon (Figure D-3). Allow to dry. Cut off the excess ribbon around each petal. Use five petals to make one flower. Place them in a circular fashion (Figure D-4). Secure the petals together with florist tape. Glue a ball fringe in the center of each flower. Bend the petals any way you wish.

Rattan Mats: Paint the mats with one coat of white household ceiling paint to "seal" the rattan. When dry, spray both mats with white enamel paint. Be sure that the mats are covered thoroughly so that they are a brilliant white. Also spray one-third of the back of the 12″ mat. When the mat is dry, fold the painted part upward. Cut a 4″ x 2½″ piece of 2″ Styrofoam and insert it into the fold. Place the red fabric over the lower part of the Styrofoam, so that the latter isn't visible through the openings of the mat. To hold the entire section together, loop a wire from the front of the mat through the Styrofoam and into the back of the mat. Twist the ends securely (Figure E).

E

F-1

F-2

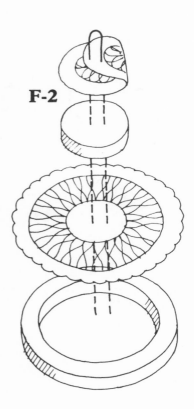

General Directions

1. Cut approximately 4″ to 5″ lengths of pine, hemlock, or greens. Starting on the side of the wreath, insert the greens, facing them outward at a slight angle.

Note: It is easier to insert the greens if you make a sharp cut on an angle at the end of each stem. If the greens do not remain securely in the wreaths, place them on 3″ picks. After you cover the entire sides with greens, cut additional 3″ to 4″ pieces of pine. Place these on top of the wreath, facing outward (and slightly inward from the edge of the other greens). Secure these greens to the wreath by placing hairpins (or heavy wire in a loop shape) over the stems.

2. Cut the polka dot ribbon lengthwise in half. Weave the ribbon through the edges of the 16″ mat. Place the mat evenly over the wreath. Securely wire the mat to the wreath (F-1). Place the green Styrofoam circle in the center of the 16″ mat (F-2). Place the 12″ folded mat on top of the Styrofoam block. Loop a wire from the front of the 12″ mat through the block and into the back of the 16″ mat (F-2). Twist the wire securely in back.

3. Fill the 12″ mat with small pieces of greens, allowing the scalloped edges of the mat to be clearly seen. Next insert pieces of greens in the circle, following the inside circular pattern of the 16″ mat. Do not hide the scalloped edges of the mat with the greens.

4. To fill the small mat, use 11 cherry balls, 5 peppermint sticks, 6 polka dot flowers, and 9 Lifesavers. Place all candies on 3″ picks or round toothpicks. Secure firmly with floral tape. Insert candies as shown.

5. To complete the outside wreath, place the twelve peppermint sticks on 4″ picks. Secure

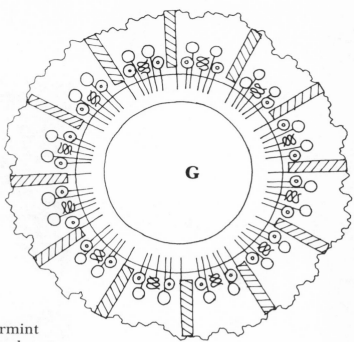

with floral tape. Insert the peppermint sticks into the wreath in clock number position. Place two Lifesavers beneath each peppermint stick. Insert the 4″ chenille stem directly into the Styrofoam. Next, insert one ribbon candy between the two Life-savers. Place each of the 24 wired cherry balls on round toothpicks or 3″ picks. Secure firmly together with floral tape. Place two cherry balls between and above the two Life-savers (Figure G).

(*Optional:* With the remaining ¾″ polka dot ribbon, make twelve small single loop bows. Place one bow at the base of each peppermint stick.)

6. Use the remaining 1½″-wide grosgrain ribbon to make a butterfly bow with long streamers. Attach the bow to the center of the small mat. Glue cherry balls on the end of the ribbon streamers and into the center of the bow.

7. To hang your design, wrap a wire around the top of the wreath. Twist the ends together securely. (Now you can sit back and admire your masterpiece.)

CANE BASKETS

MATERIALS

½"-wide masking tape
Small to medium mesh cane
White spray enamel paint
Styrofoam block to fit each basket
Trims, berries, and candies (see "Peppermint and Cherries Jubilee," p. 145.
3" florist picks or round toothpicks
Red and white chenille stems for candy canes
Empty ribbon or gift-wrap roll, 3½" diameter

Hacksaw
Corrugated cardboard
Heavy wire
Floral glue
White trim, satin cording, braid ribbon, or twine
White housepaint
Compass
Heavy posterboard
Stapler
Thin wire
Artificial boxwood or tea leaf greens
Straw Trivets

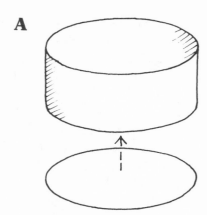

A

B

Round Basket

1. Make the base of the round basket from an empty ribbon or gift-wrap roll. Use a hacksaw to cut a 1½″ length.

2. Cut a cardboard circle to fit tightly inside the ribbon roll (Figure A). This is the bottom of the basket. Secure the cardboard circle to the roll by placing masking tape inside the basket along the seam.

3. For the handle, cut two 10″ x ¾″ strips of cane, keeping the circle design of the cane in the center of the strip (Figure B). Apply masking tape to the back of each strip before you cut them to keep them from unraveling.

4. Place the taped sides of the two strips back to back. Insert an 11″ length of heavy wire between the two strips. Place some glue between the two strips and press down firmly until the two pieces are bound tightly. When the handle is completely dry, staple both ends of the handle to the inside of the basket (Figure C).

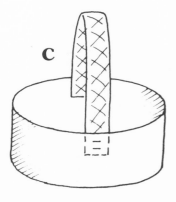

C

5. Cut a 13″ x 1½″ strip of cane. Don't forget to tape it. Wrap this piece of cane around the cardboard cylinder. The ends of the cane should meet evenly. If not, simply trim the cane until both ends are even. Glue the cane to the cylinder.

6. Glue the ½″ trim, cording, braid, or twine around the base of the basket. Paint the basket with one coat of any kind of white housepaint to seal the cardboard and cane. When dry, spray with one coat of white spray paint.

Note: I used inexpensive straw trivets that are rolled into coils for the trim on these baskets. To roll into coils, simply cut the strings and the straw coils will unroll. The strips are approximately ½″ in width.

1. Place masking tape on the cane on top of the pattern outline before you cut the cane. This keeps the cane from unraveling. Do not remove the tape from the cane after you cut it. When each basket is complete, spray with two coats of white enamel paint. When dry, glue a small piece of Styrofoam to each basket. Fill the basket first with cut-up pieces of greens, creating the shape you desire. Insert trims, berries, and candies, using 3″ florist picks or round toothpicks. (I used miniature plastic grape clusters in my baskets.) Remove all the grapes and use them singly as berries. Make candy canes by twisting together red and white chenille stems. Cut them in 3″ to 4″ segments and shape them.

Pedestal Basket

1. With a compass make a circle 5½" in diameter on the back of the cane. Tape the circle edges carefully with masking tape before cutting. Retrace the circle line on the tape. Cut out the circle. Do not remove the tape.

2. For the basket handle, see instructions for "Round Basket," p. 153.

3. For the pedestal, cut a 6½" x 2½" section from the cane. Place tape on the back along the edges before cutting. Roll the cane into a circle. Secure the two ends of the cane together with a strip of masking tape inside the circle. You can also glue or staple the edges together.

Alternative: The pedestal can be made in another way. Glue the cane to a thin fabric or aluminum foil cardboard roll (1½″ in diameter). This type of pedestal provides more support, and assembly is quicker and easier. The only disadvantage is that you cannot see through the delicate canework of the pedestal base.

4. To assemble the entire basket, staple the handle to opposite sides of the circle (Figure A). Notice that the basket is spread out. To close in the basket, bend the wire handle upward. Place a small piece of wire between both ends of the handle to hold the upper part of the basket together.

5. Glue the pedestal to the bottom of the basket (Figure B). Glue two layers of braid, cording, or twine one on top of the other, along the base of the pedestal.

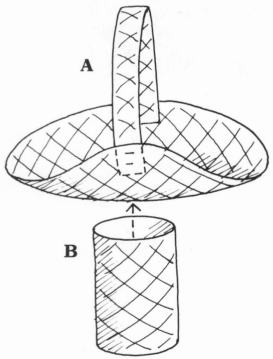

A

B

Round Mat

1. Use a compass to trace a 5½″ circle on the back of the cane. Cover the circle edges neatly with masking tape before cutting. Retrace the circle on the tape if necessary. Cut the circle but do not remove the tape.

2. Spray the entire front, and one third of the back with white enamel paint. When the mat is completely dry, fold the painted part of the circle upright (Figure A).

3. Insert a small piece of Styrofoam, 1½″ square, into the fold (Figure B). Loop a thin wire from the front of the mat through the Styrofoam and into the back of the mat. Twist the wire securely in back.

4. Fill with greens and trims. You might have to cut some of the boxwood greens in half and glue them to the Styrofoam. Be careful not to cover the lattice-work edges of mat.

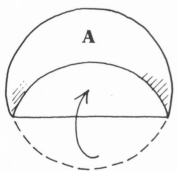

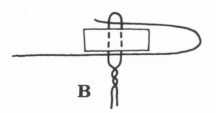

Square Basket

1. Make a small box from heavy poster-board by cutting a 7½″ x 6″ rectangle (Figure A).

2. Follow the pattern and cut slits on the heavy black lines.

3. Bend the cardboard on the dotted line. Form the box by bending the four sides upward. Staple the box securely (Figure B).

4. For the handle, see instructions for "Round Basket," p. 153. Staple the ends of the completed handle to the center of each 7½″ side.

5. Cut a 13″ x 1⅓″ strip of cane to cover the basket. Tape masking tape along the edges of the cane before you cut to prevent unraveling. Glue the can firmly to the cardboard. Crease the cane at the corners of the basket. Paint the entire basket.

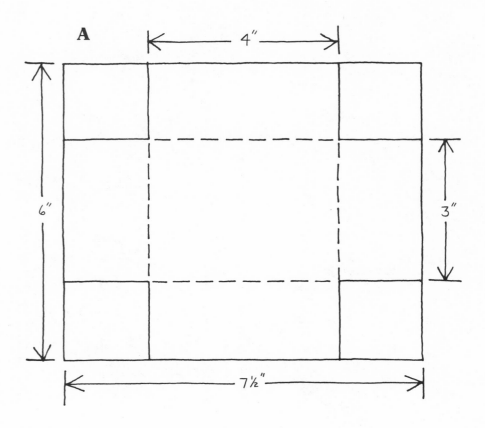

A

4"

6"

3"

7½"

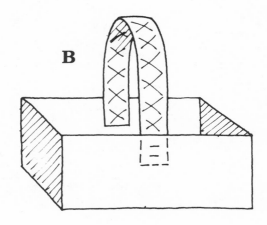

B

160

FABULOUS FAKES: OLD-FASHIONED GOODIES

See also color plate 25

MATERIALS

Creative clay (see recipe, p. 145.
Rolling pin
1¼"-diameter plastic pill bottle
Spatula
Waxed paper
Round toothpicks
Thin red corduroy
2 yards 1½"-wide peppermint stripe cotton ribbon
Floral glue
15 moss green chenille stems
15 Styrofoam balls (in assorted sizes 1" to 1½")
Clear drying glue
Nonpareils
Spray varnish
1"-thick Styrofoam
Hacksaw
5 thin dowels or pencils for lollipop sticks
30 thin beverage straws
Cranberry-colored paint
one 36"-long wooden dowel, ½" diameter (available in any lumber store)
3½ yards ⅝"-wide candy stripe grosgrain ribbon
Red paint
10"-diameter Easter basket (or any other basket)—half a basket if you wish to hang it on a wall
White spray paint
Styrofoam to fill the basket
Real or artificial greens
Assorted-size florist picks
Green floral tape
1½ yards 1½"-wide red cotton polka dot or striped grosgrain ribbon

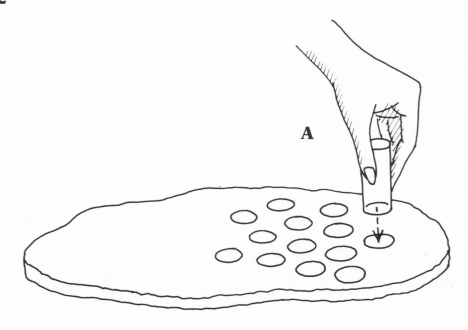

A

Make "Creative Clay," following instructions in "Peppermint and Cherries Jubilee," p. 145.

Marshmallows: Roll the clay approximately ¾" to 1" thick with a rolling pin. The top of the clay should be smooth and even. Cut out the marshmallows with the open end of the pill bottle (Figure A). Make 11 to 15 marshmallows. Remove them with a spatula and place them on waxed paper. Avoid touching the marshmallows with your fingers. When they have hardened slightly (in about two hours) turn them over and carefully insert a round toothpick halfway into the back of each one. When the marshmallows are completely dry, you may have to glue some of the toothpicks in place.

Ribbon Candy: Cut 9 to 11 12″ lengths of ½″-wide striped grosgrain ribbon. Loop the ribbon back and forth (Figure B), placing a small dab of floral glue on the alternate loops. Cut 4″ pieces of chenille stems. Glue each chenille stem along the back of the ribbon candy. The green chenille stems won't be visible when placed among the greens in the basket.

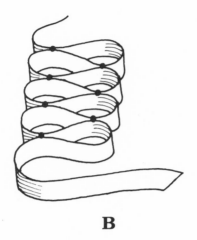

B

Nonpareil Balls: Cut 3″ chenille stems and insert them into each Styrofoam ball. Cover the balls with a thin, even coat of clear-drying glue. Use your fingers for best results. Dip the coated balls into nonpareils. When the balls are dry, lightly spray them with one coat of spray varnish. The varnish is optional but it helps to preserve the balls for three to five years. You can also use old, small wired glass-ball ornaments in place of Styrofoam balls. Use 11 to 15 balls.

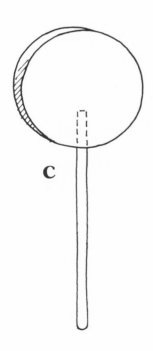

C

Lollipops: Trace 2″ circles on the 1″-thick Styrofoam. With a hacksaw cut out the circles very carefully. Next, cut the circles in half, so that two ½″-thick lollipops are formed (Figure C). If the edges of the lollipops are ragged, use a scrap of Styrofoam to sand the edges. Cover the entire lollipop with a thin coat of clear-drying glue. Use your fingers. Dip the lollipops into the nonpareils. When they are dry, glue in a white dowel or drinking straw for the lollipop stick. Make five to nine lollipops.

Licorice: Use floral glue to glue seven thin milk straws together with one straw in the center and six straws surrounding it (Figure D). Glue them together securely. When the straws are completely dry, cut 1″ lengths for the licorice. You might find it easier (depending on how you work) to cut the straws in 1″ segments first and then glue the seven straws together. Spray or coat each licorice with red paint. Glue a 3″ chenille stem or wire halfway through the center of the straw.

Peppermint Sticks: Cut 4″ pieces out of the ½″-diameter dowels, using a hacksaw blade. Starting from one end, wrap the 1½″-wide striped cotton ribbon diagonally around the dowel (Figure E). Overlap the ribbon as little as possible. Place a small dab of floral glue at the end of the dowel to hold the ribbon firmly in place. Cut off the excess ribbon at the top and the bottom. Paint the top of the dowel with red paint.

Balls: To cover balls with corduroy, see "Peppermint and Cherries Jubilee," p. 147. Make between five and nine balls.

D

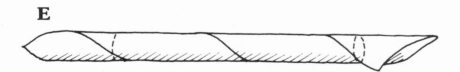

E

Assembly

1. To assemble the entire basket, fill the basket with pieces of Styrofoam. Insert pieces of hemlock and pine into the Styrofoam, creating the basic design. Use the handle of your basket as a guideline for the sphere shape. It may also be necessary to place your greens on assorted-size florist picks to hold them securely into the Styrofoam to create your design. Cover the wires from the picks and the stem of the greens with floral tape.

2. Before you place the candy into the bouquet, put each item on a florist pick, and cover the exposed wires with floral tape. (To get additional height for the candy at the top of the basket, wire one pick on top of another pick.)

3. To fill in the basket, start from the top of the centerpiece and work your way down. Insert lollipops first, then marshmallows, nonpareil balls, peppermint sticks, ribbon candy, gumdrops, and licorice. Make a butterfly bow with streamers with the cotton polka dot ribbon.

Note: You can insert some real candy as an extra treat. You can also create this same bouquet entirely with fresh candy. Simply place the candy on 8″ to 10″ toothpicks (available in the gourmet department of your grocery store) in place of the florist picks. As a sanitary precaution, cover the exposed candy with cellophane or plastic wrap twisted tightly into place.

PAPER AND LACE

See also color plate 6

MATERIALS

70 cream-colored chenille stems or 140 pipe cleaners (if only white chenille or pipe cleaners are available, you can tint them by spraying them lightly with spray shellac)

1 yard cream-colored cotton lace (or white lace tinted with instant coffee)

Thin- and medium-gauge wire

Clear-drying glue

Scissors

White floral tape

Thin cardboard

1 or 2 large sheets tan mock velvet or velour paper (available in most art stores)—or use velveteen if you wish

Stapler

¼ yard cream-colored crushed upholstery fabric (that will not shed when cut)

Florist's or baker's white satin waterproof leaves

Instant coffee

16"-diameter Styrofoam wreath

3" florist picks

3 yards 1½" cream-colored velvet ribbon

White floral buttons

Dried gypsophila (baby's breath)

Floral glue

1. Cut 45 chenille stems in half (or use 90 6″-long pipe cleaners). With each 6″ segment, make a petal by bringing the two ends together. Wrap a 5″ length of thin wire around the two ends, allowing the excess wire to hang (Figure A). Slightly flatten the rounded top part of the petal by placing your first two fingers through the center of the petal and lifting them upward. The top of the petal should now be almost square (Figure B).

2. Pour some clear-drying glue on a cardboard scrap. Place one side of the chenille petal into the glue. Pat off the excess on the cardboard. Cut strips of lace approximately 3½″ wide. Place each petal on the lace, creating rows as you go along (Figure C). When all the petals are dry, trim the lace evenly and neatly along the edges of the petals with sharp scissors. To form a flower, place three petals together. Twist the wires together securely and cover with floral tape. Place your finger lengthwise down the center of each petal. Bend the petal around your finger to create a "valley" in the center of each petal.

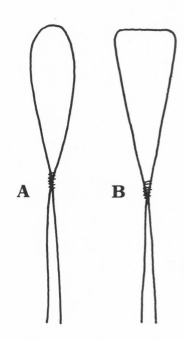

A   B

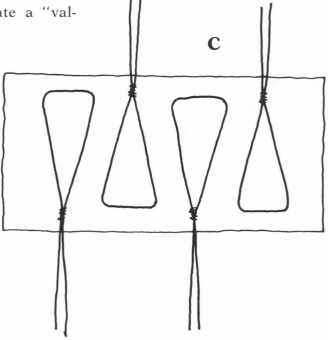

C

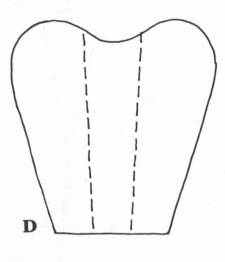

D

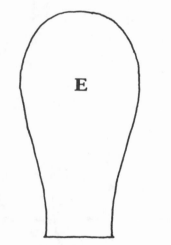

E

3. Trace the flock petal pattern onto the piece of thin cardboard (Figure D). Cut out the pattern. Using an entire sheet of velour paper to make as many petals as you can, cut all the petals. At the lower end of each petal, make a small pleat on each side so that a "valley" is created in the center of the petal. Staple the pleat together. Wrap a thin wire around the pleat at the bottom. Secure the wire with floral tape.

4. Trace the rounded upholstery petal pattern onto a thin piece of cardboard (Figure E). Cut out the pattern. Using approximately half of the crushed-velvet upholstery fabric, trace and cut out as many petals as possible. Cut 4″ chenille sections. Glue each section down the back of each petal from the top to the base of the petal.

5. Place the waterproof satin leaves in instant coffee for five minutes. The more coffee you use, the darker the leaves become. Rinse immediately with water.

6. Cut all the remaining lace into 4″ squares. Pleat the lace squares diagonally like a pinwheel (Figure F). Wrap a medium wire through the center of each square, twisting the wire in back (Figure G). Soaking some of these squares in coffee gives the wreath more variations in shading.

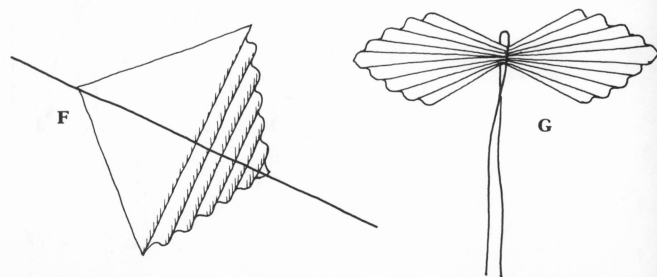

F

G

Assembly

1. To assemble the clusters, use a completed lace flower as the center of the cluster (Figure H). Below it, place three satin leaves, slightly extending beyond the flower. Cover the stems with floral tape as you go along. Add three crushed-velvet leaves slightly below the satin leaves. Each set of petals that you add should fill in the spaces from the preceding layer. Secure with floral tape. Add four velour leaves below the crushed-velvet leaves. Cover with floral tape. Finally, place two lace pinwheels under the four velour leaves. Do not congest each cluster of leaves by placing them all on the same level. Each new set of petals should be slightly underneath the other. Each cluster, when complete, should be 2″ to 2½″ in depth (from the top of the flower to the lace pinwheel) and approximately 4½″ square. Make nine to ten clusters. Cut all the stems of each cluster to a point and wrap with floral tape.

2. To assemble the entire wreath, glue and insert the clusters on the top part of the Styrofoam form, spacing them evenly (Figure I).

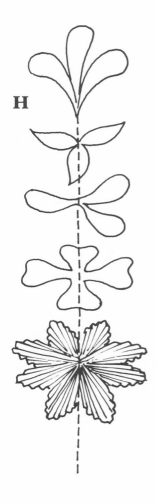

H

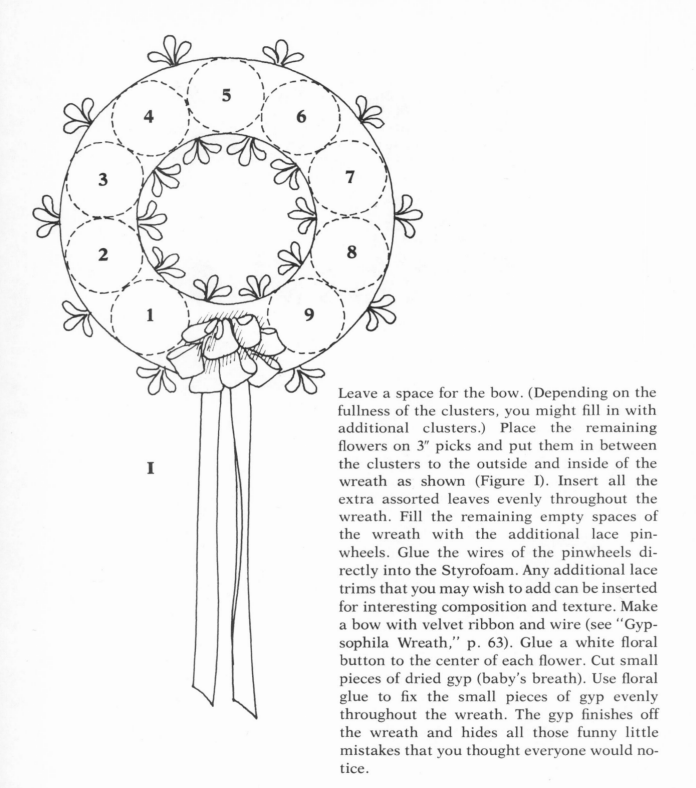

I

Leave a space for the bow. (Depending on the fullness of the clusters, you might fill in with additional clusters.) Place the remaining flowers on 3″ picks and put them in between the clusters to the outside and inside of the wreath as shown (Figure I). Insert all the extra assorted leaves evenly throughout the wreath. Fill the remaining empty spaces of the wreath with the additional lace pinwheels. Glue the wires of the pinwheels directly into the Styrofoam. Any additional lace trims that you may wish to add can be inserted for interesting composition and texture. Make a bow with velvet ribbon and wire (see "Gypsophila Wreath," p. 63). Glue a white floral button to the center of each flower. Cut small pieces of dried gyp (baby's breath). Use floral glue to fix the small pieces of gyp evenly throughout the wreath. The gyp finishes off the wreath and hides all those funny little mistakes that you thought everyone would notice.

MATCHING BOUQUET

See also color plate 6

MATERIALS

Medium- and heavy-gauge wire	Wire cutter
14 lace flowers	Fine natural-colored dried stems
Flocked and satin leaves	such as wheat or pond grass
White floral tape	1½″ wide cream-colored velvet
Dried gypsophila (baby's breath)	ribbon

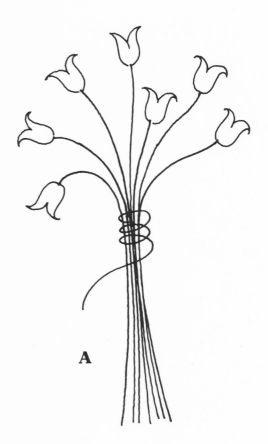

A

1. Cut 7″ lengths of heavy wire. In order to lengthen stems of the flowers and the assorted petals, place a wire adjacent to the stem of each item. Secure the stem to the wire firmly with floral tape.

2. Make seven clusters of gyp (baby's breath). Cut 10″ lengths of wire and wrap them around the stems of the gyp but leave 6″ of the wire free. Cover the wire and stems securely with floral tape.

3. To assemble the bouquet, place the flowers together in a free-style arrangement, bringing the stems together (Figure A). Wrap a wire around the stems to hold the bouquet firmly together.

4. Once you have achieved the desired shape, insert seven clusters of gyp (Figure B). The gyp provides body for your bouquet, and prevents the flowers and petals from drooping or moving around. Tape the wires from the gyp securely to the bouquet. Fill in the bouquet with the assorted wired leaves and petals. Wrap a wire around all the stems of the bouquet. Cover with floral tape.

5. Cut all the hanging stems and wires with a pair of wire cutters, leaving a 1″ nub. Be careful not to cut above the point where all the stems come together (Figure C).

6. Make three separate clusters of dried stems. To hold the stems of each cluster together, wrap floral tape tightly around the top of each cluster. Place the clusters over the nub, covering as much of the nub as possible. Secure the stems to the nub with floral tape (Figure C). Glue additional

stems fanning upward from the nub into the bouquet to give the appearance of the stems coming from the flowers.

7. Make a single loop bow from the velvet ribbon. Wrap the wire from the bow around the entire nub to conceal the floral tape around the nub. Gently spread the stems by bending them upward and outward. Cut the stems unevenly to give a more natural appearance to the finished bouquets.

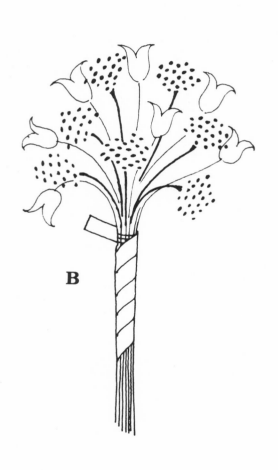

B

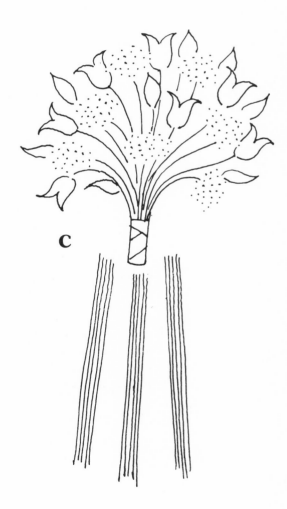

C

GINGHAM FIRESIDE BROOM

See also color plate 5

MATERIALS

8 white chenille stems
9 1"-diameter Sytrofoam balls
Medium wire
Floral tape
Artificial or real pine
Floral glue
2½ yards of ½"-wide gingham ribbon

2½ yards 1½"-wide double-edge eyelet
Masking tape
White silk, cloth, dried flowers or other materials as a color accent
2½ yards 1½"-wide red satin, cotton, velvet, or grosgrain ribbon
½ yard tiny white ball fringe

174

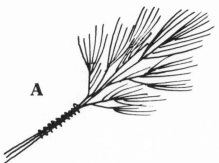

A

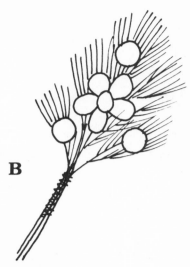

B

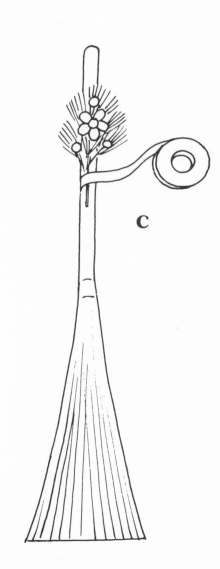

C

1. To make the three gingham flowers, see "Paper and Lace Wreath," page 167. Substitute gingham fabric for the lace and use five petals to make each flower.

2. Cut nine 4″ squares from the remaining gingham fabric. Place a Styrofoam ball in the center. (See "Peppermint and Cherries Jubilee," p. 147). Pull the four corners together. Twist the excess tightly in back. Wrap a 9″ length of medium-gauge wire around the twist, leaving 4″ of wire free. Cover the entire twist with floral tape.

3. Make three separate clusters of pine, 4″ to 5″ in length (Figure A). Secure the stem of each cluster together with wire. Cover the wire with floral tape.

4. Into each cluster of pine, insert one flower and three covered balls (Figure B). Space them evenly. Twist all the stems in the cluster together and cover with floral tape.

5. To assemble, place the first cluster on the upper third of the broom, facing upward (Figure C). Attach the cluster to the broom by wrapping masking tape around the wires of the cluster and the handle of the broom.

6. Leave a 1½″ space below the first cluster, where the ribbon will be inserted later. Place two more clusters below this space,

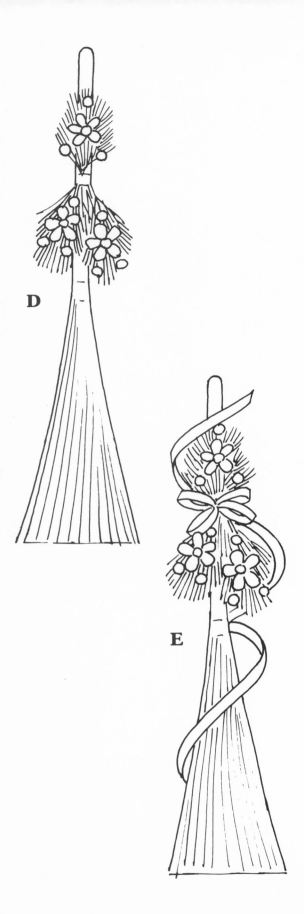

D

E

facing downward, one below the other (Figure D). Again, wrap masking tape around the two remaining clusters to the broom to hold them securely in place.

7. Glue the gingham ribbon lengthwise down the center of the eyelet. Cut a 2½-yard length of medium wire. Place the wire down the center of a 2½-yard strip of masking tape. Attach the wired tape to the back of the satin or grosgrain ribbon. Glue the eyelet to the wired ribbon so that the back of the eyelet is red.

8. Make a butterfly bow (see page 28). Cut off the excess ribbon and use it as the streamer.

9. At a point one third the distance from the left end of the streamer, wire the bow to the streamer.

10. Place the bow, on a slight diagonal, into the 1½" space on the broom (Figure E). Secure the bow to the handle with wire. Loop and weave the streamer throughout the bouquet and the broom. Place a small amount of glue at each fold or twist of the ribbon to hold it securely in place.

11. Glue a ball fringe, cloth flowers, and small pieces of dried materials on the pine throughout the bouquet.

VICTORIAN BLUE WREATH

See also color plate 2

MATERIALS

12″ x 24″ piece 1″-thick Styrofoam
Hacksaw or serrated knife
½ yard striped tapestry fabric (stripe is about 1½″)
Straight pins
7 to 9 yards 1″-wide gray blue velvet ribbon
4 green chenille stems
5 2″-diameter Styrofoam balls
2 yards cream-colored upholstery gimp (available in fabric stores that carry upholstery fabrics)

Floral glue
Scissors
3″ and 4″ florist picks
16″-diameter Styrofoam wreath
Dried gypsophila (baby's breath)
Real or artificial pine and evergreens
Dried gray eucalyptus (If you can't purchase dried eucalyptus, buy 1 or 2 fresh pieces. Hang them upside down in a cool place until they dry.)

A

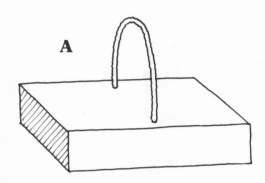

B

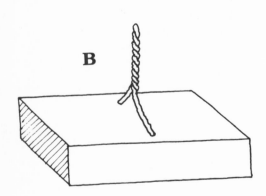

1. Cut seven 4″ x 2½″ pieces from the Styrofoam with a hacksaw or serrated knife.

2. Cut strips from the striped tapestry leaving a ½″ excess on either side of the stripe. Cover the entire top and sides of the packages with tapestry fabric, leaving a little more than three quarters of the back uncovered. Secure the fabric to the Styrofoam with straight pins. Vary the tapestry strips by placing them horizontally, vertically, side by side, etc. Pin the velvet ribbon along the edges of each package on either side of the tapestry stripe.

3. Cut 4″ lengths of chenille stem. Glue and insert the ends of the chenille stem 2″ apart in the back of each package (Figure A). Twist the center of the chenille loop so that it can be attached easily to a florist pick (Figure B).

4. The method of covering the 2″ Styrofoam balls you use depends on the width of the tapestry stripe (avoid stripes wider than 1½″ since it is difficult to cover the balls). You have to cover only one half the ball, because the other half is tucked into the wreath and won't be visible. Carefully cut the stripes from your fabric: cut two lengths to fit from the top half to the bottom half of the ball.

5. Glue one stripe to the ball (Figure C). Stretch the fabric tightly to keep as wrinkle-free as possible. Cut off with scissors any small wrinkles or bumps along the edges.

6. Apply the second stripe adjacent to the first stripe. The upper and lower parts of this stripe should overlap the first stripe (Fig-

ure D). Simply cut and trim the overlap so that the first stripe is flush with the second.

7. Glue the upholstery gimp over the seam of the two stripes, continuing around the ball (Figure E). Glue a 3″ chenille stem to the back of the ball and attach to a florist pick.

Note: You can make your own wreath, using a Styrofoam form. Another option is to purchase a ready-made evergreen wreath and wire or glue the accessories to the wreath. The ready-made wreath won't give the same fullness and thickness as a Styrofoam wreath, however.

Assembly

1. Make an evergreen wreath (see p. 24). Any of the three procedures work well. (I used a Styrofoam form to obtain extra depth and fullness.) Place the chenille stems from the packages and balls on picks and insert into the wreath.

2. To make the tapestry bow, cut seven 10″ strips and two 14″ strips of striped tapestry fabric. The width of each strip should be 2½″, with the tapestry stripe in the center.
Note: If your fabric appears to unravel easily after cutting, you can make your strips 3½″ wide. Fold back ½″ on either side along the edges. Glue or sew the seam in place. This will also make a more finished ribbon.

3. Glue the velvet ribbon to both sides of the tapestry stripe. Follow the same procedure on all nine strips. Next, form a loop with each 10″ strip by pinching the ends together and placing securely on 3″ picks.

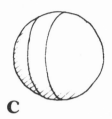

C

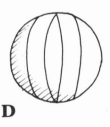

D

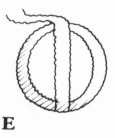

E

4. Insert five loops into the Styrofoam in a circular pattern. Place the two remaining loops in the center of the circle. Place the two 14″ strips on picks and suspend them as streamers from the bow.

5. Glue small clusters of gyp (baby's breath) to the greens, placing them evenly over the wreath.

6. Place small pieces of eucalyptus on 3″ picks and insert throughout any spaces that remain.

7. Cut seven 12″ lengths of velvet ribbon. Make single cross bows in the middle of each piece. Place the bows on picks and insert them throughout the wreath. Weave the streamers gracefully among the pine and gyp, using glue to hold them securely in place.

VICTORIAN BLUE TREE ORNAMENT

See also color plate 21

MATERIALS:

Striped tapestry fabric to cover balls	2¾″-diameter Styrofoam balls
	Floral glue
1″-wide blue velvet ribbons to trim balls	Straight pins
	Scissors

1. Cut six 5″ lengths of tapestry strips. Cover the entire Styrofoam ball with these strips. Follow the same procedure as with the small balls in the "Victorian Blue Wreath." p. 178.

2. Fold the velvet ribbon in half and glue the seam together.

3. Cover the seams of the ball with the doubled velvet ribbon. (You can use upholstery gimp instead.) Glue or pin the ribbon in place.

4. Make small bows for the top and the bottom of the ball with the doubled ribbon. Secure in place with straight pins.

5. Form a loop for hanging. Attach the loop to the ball in the center of the bow with a long straight pin or hat pin.

VICTORIAN BLUE CENTERPIECE

See also color plate 1

MATERIALS

8 4″ x 2⅔″ pieces of 1″-thick Styrofoam (Vary the sizes slightly)

4 yards ⅜″-wide velvet ribbon

2⅔ yards ⅝″-wide velvet ribbon

⅛ yard striped tapestry fabric (stripe should be no wider than 1½″) or 3½ yards tapestry-like ribbon with approximately 1½″-wide stripe

Scissors

2 pieces 1″-thick Styrofoam, 4″ x 8″ and 2″ x 2″

1 piece 3″ x 6″ 2″-thick Styrofoam

Artificial or real pine and greens

Dried gypsophila (baby's breath)

Floral glue

3 18″-long candles

3 candle holders (plastic or metal) available in dime stores

Assorted-size florist picks

8 pipe cleaners

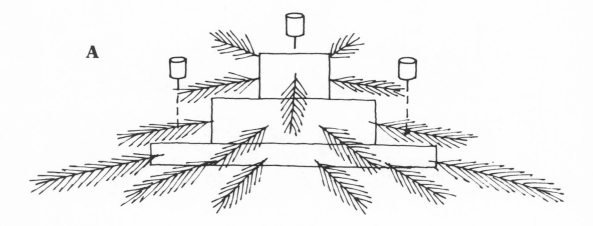

A

1. Cover the eight packages as in "Victorian Blue Wreath," p. 178. To make the ribbon, cut your striped tapestry fabric into the strips, leaving a ½" seam on both sides of the stripe. Cut strips into 7" lengths. With the remaining ribbon, cut four identical lengths for the streamers. Carefully glue the ⅜"-wide ribbon along the ¼" seams on both sides of the tapestry stripe.

2. To make the foundation, glue the 2" square Styrofoam to the center of the 3" x 6" piece. Glue the 3" x 6" piece to the center of the 4" x 8" piece. Cut pieces of pine and evergreens. Place the greens on 3", 4", or 6" florist picks and insert them into the Styrofoam, slanting downward at an angle (Figure A). Make an oval shape. Once you have achieved the basic shape you can add smaller pieces of pine, extending upward and outward. Do not proceed until you are satisfied with the complete foundation.

1. Insert the candle holders into the 2″ square Styrofoam; one in the center and one on either side of the center. Insert the candles into the holders. Form a loop with each pipe cleaner and glue the ends, ½″ apart, to the back of the Styrofoam packages. Twist the loop. Placing the loops on 4″ or 6″ florist picks and insert into the Styrofoam (as shown).

2. Form a loop with each tapestry strip and place each loop on a 4″ pick. Put two streamers together and place one end on a 6″ florist pick. Next, insert two loops on either side of the outside candles, forming a bow. Place the streamers directly below the bow. Glue small clusters of gyp (baby's breath) and eucalyptus to the greens. *Alternative:* You could use glass chimneys or hurricane globes over your candles. Look in flea markets for some old, etched Victorian glass globes.

POPCORN AND CRANBERRY WREATH

See also color plate 7

MATERIALS

13 ½"-diameter green Styrofoam wreath (or a white wreath painted green)

Real or artificial pine, tea-leaf greens, or boxwood

Heavy, stiff green wire

Floral glue

Popcorn

Medium wire

Real or artificial cranberries (You can also make your own cranberries from "Creative Clay" (p. 145) by making small balls, inserting the heavy wire while they are still wet, and allowing them to dry. Paint them red.)

3 yards red velvet tubing

Dried gypsophila (baby's breath)

A-1

A-2

1. Cover your wreath with greens. You can use any of the three methods described in Chapter 1 to cover the wreath (Figures A-1, A-2, and A-3). I used a tea-leaf garland to wrap around the frame of this Styrofoam wreath.

2. Glue a 3″ to 4″ length of heavy wire through the center of each cranberry and each popcorn. When the glue is dry, glue the wires from the popcorn and cranberries directly to the Styrofoam. Place the berries one at a time or in clusters of three. Add as many of each as you desire.

3. For the bow, insert medium wire through the velvet tubing. Make a larger bow for the center and three smaller bows for the top and sides. Add a streamer to each of the bows but do not add any wire inside. Knot the ends of the streamers.

4. Place the bows on 3″ picks and insert into the Styrofoam.

5. Glue small pieces of gypsophila (baby's breath) to the greens evenly over the wreath.

A-3

POPCORN AND CRANBERRY BOUQUET

See also color plate 18

MATERIALS

36–48 3″ artificial boxwood or tealeaf greens
2¾″-diameter Styrofoam ball
Stiff wire
Popcorn
Cranberries

Floral glue
1½ yards red velvet tubing
Dried gypsophila (baby's breath)
Small basket or bushel, 6″ diameter
Scissors

1. Insert 3″ artificial boxwood picks into the Styrofoam ball. Cover two-thirds to three-fourths of the ball with them.

2. Use the same wiring procedure as for "Popcorn and Cranberry Wreath," p. 187. Glue the completed items evenly to the Styrofoam ball (Figure A).

3. Next, add two small bows made of the velvet tubing—one in front and one in the back of the bouquet. Knot the ends of the streamers.

4. Glue small pieces of gypsophila (baby's breath) evenly over the bouquet.

5. Place bouquet in basket. Support with extra Styrofoam if desired.

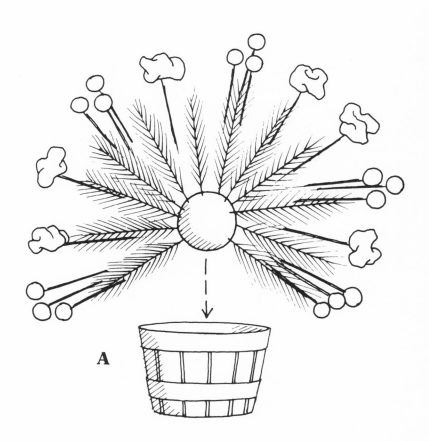

A

A

NOSEGAY

See also color plate 18

MATERIALS

Same materials as for "Popcorn and Cranberry Bouquet," p. 188, plus 2"-wide cream-colored lace or eyelet and a 1"-diameter Styrofoam ball.

1. Cut the boxwood or tea leaf greens in half so that each piece is 1" long.
2. Glue the cut greens to the Styrofoam ball, covering only one half the ball (Figure A).
3. Glue the popcorn and cranberries directly to the greens.
4. Make a ruffle with the cream-colored lace around the blank half of the Styrofoam ball, forming a doily. Glue into place. Add a velvet-tubing bow. Glue a 3" pick to the back of the nosegay to make it easier to attach the ornament to your tree.

TREE BASKET

See also color plate 18

Cut up small pieces of greens as for "Nosegay." Place a small block of Styrofoam in a miniature basket and fill as above.

FIVE

How To Make What Looks Good Look Even Better

Now WHAT TO DO with your fabulous creation? After the design itself, I consider merchandising—that is, effectively displaying your design—the most important thing. Basically what merchandising involves is creating a pretty picture, using complementary accessories and arranging them effectively around your focus point to create an attractive collection. You may call it styling or interior design, but whatever you call it, it makes what looks good look even better. And that's not all. It makes what looks bad look better. You just can't lose.

WHERE TO PUT IT

Placing your design in a strategic location can create a more effective setting. Before you undertake a particular project, you should have an idea of where you want to put it. Putting something that looks good in the wrong place can spoil its effectiveness. Most designs in

191

this book can be easily adapted to suit your interior simply by changing the colors that were used in the samples to colors that fit into your home.

Put the completed design in a place of importance in your room—over a fireplace, on a kitchen, dining-room, or coffee table, buffet or sideboard, in an archway, and so on—in short, on any important piece of furniture in your room or on any interesting or important architectural structure. Placing an object on a focus wall (the main wall that you see when you first walk into a room) enhances that object. An important part of merchandising is composition—the pattern in which your accessories are arranged. I have found that arranging accessories in groupings or "collections" makes for more interesting composition. Place things in a cluster and see for yourself. Usually the "one on this side, one on that side" arrangement creates a rather stiff, stagnant, or formal composition. When you put accessories around your display, try to group items in odd numbers—three, five, seven, or nine. Good composition usually works best with an odd number of objects. Experiment, it's the best experience.

LIGHTING

How effectively you light your display determines the mood or atmosphere you create for your design. Dramatic lighting is always impressive. A good example of dramatic lighting is to use a single-focus spotlight and place it to the side of, underneath, or directly over your focus point. This creates dramatic shadows.

Note: Lighting placed to the side highlights and complements rough textures. It also "reinforces" the shape or design and creates depth. Unfortunately, side lighting also "highlights" sloppy seams, uneven spheres, or obvious flaws in workmanship. On the other hand, lighting placed in the front hides most of the sloppy seams, uneven spheres, and obvious flaws, but it also tends to make your design somewhat flat looking, eliminating most texture and depth. You may then decide to use a combination of both lighting positions for best results. Ten or fifteen candles, effectively arranged and lighted around your display, is another type of dramatic lighting. Candle-

192

light radiates a warm glow and can be most effective. Experiment with light to find out how much more interesting you can make your display.

COLOR

Good color combinations are important to good design. A good design, executed in uninteresting colors, is ordinary and the design will tend to seem—however unjustly—average. On the other hand, if the design is not outstanding but the use of color is, the appealing colors will carry the design.

Here is a list of some attractive and unusual color combinations that you may wish to incorporate into your designs or into the color scheme of your home.

Kelly green, yellow, and white
White, beige, and tan
Black, brown, and cream
Putty and white
Khaki and navy
Rust, navy, and cream
Gray-blue and apricot

Burgundy and gray
Burgundy and cream
Rust and brown
Mauve and cream
Forest green, rust, and beige
Red, brown, and beige
Mauve, raspberry, and ecru

STYLE

In order to help you merchandise your design more effectively, here are descriptions of four basic styles or modes of design: Country, Victorian, Traditional, and Contemporary. Each style has its own identity and yet it can draw from any of the other styles to give it lasting appeal

It is usually difficult for a designer or anyone else to recall spontaneously the textures, designs, and accessories typically associated with a particular decorating style. It's equally important to know to which of these you have easy access. Therefore, I have compiled, for my use and yours, a list of basic accessories that are characteristic of each decorating style. I use this list constantly as a reference for display, interior design, and photo styling. With this list, you can become an instant designer. Here's how to use it.

Look at your design and decide into which decorating style it fits: Country, Victorian, Traditional, or Contemporary.

Look at the list under that decorating style for the general accessories that are compatible with that category. Rummage through your cupboards, attics, garage, and cellar—you're sure to come up with at least a few items that you can use! While color accent is important, don't forget about textures and finishes: Rough, smooth, high gloss, matte, clear, opaque, translucent, and so on. Experiment by placing the accessories in different positions until you are satisfied with a particular grouping. You may even want to mix some of the accessories from two styles, such as Traditional and Contemporary for an eclectic look. Don't be surprised if you enjoy this part more than actually making the design itself. You can spend hours and hours of enjoyment just experimenting with accessories.

Country

Country is both a feeling and a style. Many decorating styles have their own "Country"—that is, Colonial Country, Traditional Country, Contemporary Country. Generally, Country-style furnishings and accessories are simple, fresh, crisp, but not heavy—just open, light, and natural.

COUNTRY THINGS

Crockery, jugs, jars
Pewter
Quilts
Small prints
Calico
Fruit
Dried-flower materials
Ball fringe
Baskets
Milk bottles
Spices
Natural foodstuffs
Wheat, nuts
Fresh flowers

Eyelet, gingham
Ruffles
Painted finishes
Canning jars
Chicken wire
Grosgrain ribbon
Shutters
Barnwood
Cane, rush
Burlap, straw
Eggs, dairy products
Pattern on pattern
Plants
Pine

Traditional

Traditional is really a combination of many design styles, incorporating the best of what had been handed down from the past. Furniture and accessories with classic lines dominate this style. Traditional decorating tends to appear relatively formal and sophisticated.

TRADITIONAL THINGS

Antique brass
Silver
Crystal
Tapestry, velvet, satin
Needlepoint
Silk flowers
Plants
Carved wooden accessories
Porcelain
China

Oriental accessories
Bronze
Antiques
Fine linens
Paintings
Sculpture
Fine pottery
Gold leaf
Leather
Fine glass

Victorian

Victorian refers to the period from 1840 to the turn of the century that is associated with ornamentation and "gingerbread" (woodwork, scrolls, carvings, lattice works, filigree, moldings). To some people, Victorian instantly suggests clutter; there seemed to be never enough accessories or groupings to fit on a shelf or wall.

VICTORIAN THINGS

Bric-a-brac
Crystal
Pressed glass
Tapestry
Needlepoint
Damask
Fringe, trimmings, lace
Crochet work
Embroidery
Stained glass
Bevel mirrors

Turn-of-the-century oak
Bronze
Art Nouveau designs
Muted colors
Quilts
Florals
Bamboo, wicker
Tiles
Old postcards
Gingerbread and ornamentation
Black walnut

Contemporary

Contemporary is both a feeling and a style. I like to think of it as being smooth and slick. Contemporary takes lines from other design styles and simplifies them into essential forms. While it doesn't generate some of the warmth and antique charm of other styles, it certainly compensates with sparkle and immediate impact.

CONTEMPORARY THINGS

Mirror
Glass, acrylics
Chrome, brass
Grasscloth
Textures
Jute, macrame
Natural wood
Brick, terra cotta
Earth colors
Pottery
Plants

Bleached dried materials
Feathers
Baskets
Geometrics, abstracts
Seashells
Bamboo, wicker
Cane
Canvas, suede
Tortoise shell
Oriental accessories
Rocks, minerals

HOW TO BUY IT WHOLESALE

Now that you have decided you want the thrill and glitter of being a designer, you may want to begin selling your magnificent creations. Therefore, you qualify to establish yourself as a business and "buy it wholesale."

First, you'll need a state resale or tax number (you can get one through your state department for about two dollars). This number officially establishes you as a business. That's it.

Next, look through the Yellow Pages of major cities near your home. Look under "Florists, wholesale," or "hobby" for paints, wood plaques, glues, and trims. Make sure you give your business a professional sounding name. Many wholesalers do not sell to just anyone "off the street" or to "illegitimate" people who work from their homes. And be confident of what you are going to say to or ask of your suppliers.

Wholesale Buying for Organizations

If you are with a women's guild, social organization, or fund-raising club, more than likely the association has a tax-exempt number (the same as a resale number) that exempts it from paying tax on items purchased from either a retailer or a wholesaler. Simply give salespeople the tax number before they ring up your sale. You can use the tax exempt number in fabric stores, art and craft stores, lumber stores, and many others. You might even ask if they give discounts to organizations and professionals. Many wholesalers allow organizations to purchase from them. Should one wholesaler refuse you, try others.

There's only one place that's cheaper than wholesale. If you enjoy people and a good bargain, you will absolutely love tag sales, garage sales, and flea markets. No place else sells so much for so little. Wicker, Christmas supplies, unusual vases and containers, antiques, baskets, or whatever—you'll find it at tag sales. My second choice is flea markets or second-hand shops. The advantage is that you make one trip and then have a large selection to choose from the many stalls. Many dealers go to tag sales 45 minutes to an hour before the tag sale actually opens, picking out all the antiques (that you didn't know were antiques) and any merchandise that they can make money on. Then they just resell it to you. But these items still are pretty inexpensive. In fact, many of the accessories used to merchandise the design in this book came from tag sales.

All of which goes to show that no matter what you start with, whether costly, second-hand, or free, good design remains good design. And any flair that you give it makes it personal and exclusively yours.

Materials and Skills Index

General Index